≪ **Praise for**

"Vintage Hinze. If you like well... suspense with your romance, if you like clues and curves at a roller coaster pace, *Duplicity* is for you. It's a page-turner, and don't skip a page."
—*The Courier Herald*

"Clear an entire shelf for this author's work, she doesn't disappoint, making her a sure candidate for the bestseller's list. Very Highly Recommended." —*BookBrowser*

"The incredible Hinze generates a thriller of mind-blowing intensity, delivering action and suspense with an incredible punch." —*RT BOOK CLUB on Lady Justice*

"www.ArmchairInterviews has an enormous amount of respect for Hinze's ability to conjure up a scintillating read."
— *Armchair Interviews on Body Double*

"There is no question that author Vicki Hinze has delivered a tour de force thriller that will leave readers gasping for breath." —*RT Book Club on Lady Liberty*

"I have seen so much misleading or inaccurate information passed around on the web that I worry about recommending online newsletters, editors or anything else to my students. Vicki Hinze is *the* exception. She never fails to inspire, give fail-safe advice on writing and, now that *All About Writing to Sell* is available, we no longer must wait for her columns in installments." — Carolyn Howard Johnson on *All About Writing to Sell*

"An indispensable tool. Readers familiar with fabulously informative newsletter, *Aids4Writers*, will recognize [Hinze's] informative, informal style. Filled with encouragement, advice, and backstage knowledge, *All About Writing to Sell* covers the material that typically fills dozens of books on the writing craft. A must have for all authors. Very Highly Recommended."
—*Wordweaving.com*

❧ Works by Vicki Hinze ❧

Nonfiction
One Way to Write A Novel
All About Writing to Sell
The Common Sense Guide for
Writers

Festival
Maybe This Time
Mind Reader

A Message from Cupid
Seeing Fireworks

Seascape Series
Beside a Dreamswept Sea
Upon a Mystic Tide
Beyond the Misty Shore

IT GIRL series
Invitation to a Murder
Bulletproof Princess

Her Perfect Life
The Prophet's Lady

War Games series
Double Dare
Double Vision
Smokescreen:
Total Recall
Body Double

Military Novels
All Due Respect
Acts of Honor
Duplicity
Shades of Gray

Political Novels
Lady Justice
Lady Liberty

The
Common Sense
Guide
for
Writers

Vicki Hinze

Spilled Candy Books
Niceville, Florida

The Common Sense Guide for Writers
Copyright, 2006

By Vicki Hinze

Published by: Spilled Candy Books
Spilled Candy Publications
Post Office Box 5202
Niceville, FL 32578-5202
http://www.spilledcandy.com

Spilled Candy Books is committed to its authors and their work. For this reason, we do not permit our covers to be "stripped" for returns, but instead, we require that the whole book be returned in saleable condition, allowing us to resell it. Resale condition is defined as no markings, stamps, scuffs, bent covers, or any condition in which you yourself would not wish to buy the book.

ISBN: (trade paperback) 1-892718-63-4
First edition, printed June 2006
Printed in the United States of America

Cover Design: Copyright 2006
Cover Photo Credit: Linda Galloway

✧ Table of Contents ✧

✑ Introduction ❧

LIFE IS MAGNIFICENT, and it's tough.

For writers and other creative people, sometimes it's worse than tough, and when it is, our basic instincts insist we find someone else to blame.

And so we do.

We blame our publisher, our editor or agent; our spouse or kids; our in-laws, parents or siblings. We blame a cover artist, a copyeditor—or, if necessary, a rushed salesclerk, a slow-moving driver or a harried postal worker. We blame any and everyone *except* us.

But sooner or later, we realize that we're the ones working hardest at making our lives most tough, and then we're astonished.

Why do we do this to us?

More importantly...

How can we not do this to us?

Writers mirror humanity. And as humans, too often we don't talk or listen to ourselves or consciously decide what we want from life much less from our careers. We're too busy scrambling to earn a living, raising our families, trying to sell what we've written. Responsibilities constantly bombard us, and each of them cries, "Take care of me first."

We're so busy that we're stressed to our outer limits and so we do what is human...

We ignore.

We zone out rather than tune in to career choices that actively seek to manifest what we really want in our lives. And we convince ourselves that we need the refuge. The escape.

We need the rest!

But the truth is that there is no refuge.

We're not escaping from anything.

And we are not resting.

And, though we might try, we can't stay zoned out forever. Eventually, life intrudes and drags us back to it. When we are forced to return, we're no less stressed and our lives and careers are no less busy or any more harmonious or focused than they were before we tuned out the world with our "ignore it and it'll go away" attitudes and we visited the zone. So that raises the inevitable question:

What are we accomplishing by zoning out?

And that raises the inevitable answer:

Nothing.

If we're accomplishing nothing, then we're just drifting, day-to-day, year-to-year, without stopping to think about who we are (which manifests in millions of ways in our writing) or what we hope to accomplish in our work. And worse, we're practicing avoidance.

Talking to ourselves and hearing what we really think can be dangerous. We might not like what we find out. We might put ourselves in a position where we have to *do* something. God forbid, we might actually have to change.

We don't like change.

Whether it's a career decision or one that forces us to alter our perception of a belief, we fear change. It's a fact—and a natural human response. Forget whether the change is good or bad—that doesn't matter. Change is spooky. It scares the socks off us because no matter how far out of balance we feel, or how little personal harmony we enjoy, or how much stress we're under, we are more comfortable with what we know than with the unknown.

Change means different.

Different agent. Different editor. Different publishing house.

Different type of writing. Different techniques in writing. A different approach to promoting or marketing our works.

Different.

And different in any form forces us to traipse out of our known comfort zone and onto new ground. Ground we're not sure is solid. Who can say what pitfalls lurk there in the unknown, just waiting to knock us to our knees? We could fall through a crack. Expose our roots. Make a career misstep from which we'll never recover.

Who wants to risk it?

The simple truth is that we all want to risk it. We deny it—often at the top of our lungs and from the depths of our souls—but, at some point in our lives and careers, we all want more... or less.

Even though we're afraid of change, we want it. At times, we even crave it. We want more money, more perks, more fulfillment from what we're producing. We want more joy in actually performing the work, higher print runs, better distribution. We want more harmony with ourselves and others, and more security. We also want less stress, less discontent, less upset and isolation and fear.

We want balance.

We want to feel connected and purposeful. To know our works hold value. Actually, we want to know that our lives matter. That *we* matter. And we want to know that what we're writing and what we're doing matters. Oh, yes. We want change.

Typically, we think that change requires a major investment on our parts. We cringe, duck and dodge it, telling ourselves that we have no time, desire or interest in making yet another major investment or commitment—we're running ourselves ragged already. Just the idea of changing has us feeling so overwhelmed that we do nothing.

But the urges persist.

I'm sick of writing the same old stuff.

I should push the boundaries more.

I should try to write a different kind of book.

Then fear and doubt step in to debate, and they are strong and persuasive.

Sick of writing the same old stuff? You've worked for years to get where you are. Now you just want to write something different?

Are you ready to start over at square one?

In this competitive market?

You're making a decent living. Pushing the boundaries and writing something different is fine, but what if it doesn't sell? Can you afford to invest the time it'll take to write a book that might not sell? Can you justify—to yourself, your spouse, your family and friends and writing peers—spending the time to write a book that you know just has a good shot at being published but no guarantees?

Come on. Have you lost it?

Strong and persuasive.

And, we decide, these are all sensible, logical reasons not to make any changes. The urges persist, but we're armed with fear and doubt's logic and sense and reason now, so we wiggle our way around them. We rationalize through the niggles and nudges and even the cravings and we bury them under busy-ness.

But the urges come back. They always come back. Frankly, they turn into real nags.

Yet we've had a little practice now, and we put it to use. We're good at shoving these urges away, and even at denying they exist. We work hard at it, swearing there is no way that we can take on one more major project—especially one that will change us. We tell ourselves we can't risk a speculative venture—even if it excites it to the point of distraction. It's just not fair to our professional associates, who have devoted considerable resources to building our careers, or to our supporters, or to our families, who depend on our income. We just *can't* do it. It's a luxury not a necessity; one we can't afford.

We tell ourselves all that and more.

And we believe ourselves.

Well, it's time to dispel the myth. Change does *not* require anything major from us. It does require something from us: a little patience, a little common sense, and a little courage.

In this book, my mission is to offer you an opportunity to see how you can simplify your career choices—and by extension, your life—by simplifying your thinking. How you can identify who you are and decide what matters most to you.

As a summa cum laude graduates of the ***School of Hard Knocks for Writers,*** I've survived many career lessons. Those, of course, directly impact a writer's personal life, not to mention her sanity.

Often, as a requirement to personal growth, the writer must bite the bullet and take the risks. At times, she compromises. (Writes that speculative book on the side... anyway.) At other times, she just has to wing it. But if the writer acts from the vantage point of being informed, relying on training, experience, and intuition—the writer's own *and* that of other writers and professional associates—then she greatly enhances her odds for success without scraping her knees and knuckles and nose.

The writer's career road is full of potholes and pitfalls. Dangerous curves abound and yield signs are plentiful. As a new writer, you're rolling along on square wheels. As you gain experience, you round off the sharp edges.

Each personal experience acts as a **guidepost**. Guideposts better the writer's odds of living her professional and personal life with greater harmony, more peace and fewer wounds.

Who among us doesn't rejoice at the possibility of suffering fewer wounds?

Any writer or creative genius that wants a more fulfilled life can have one by thinking and making conscious decisions. By exercising a little common sense, and by summoning her own inner courage.

You supply the courage.

That's **Guidepost #1** in *The Common Sense Guide for Writers.*

◈ Guidepost 1 ❧

Courage

COURAGE IS BEING WILLING to take a stand when taking that stand isn't popular with others—with people who might, or might not, matter to you.

It's opening yourself up to criticism, tossing out your thoughts, opinions and feelings for the rest of the world to scrutinize and, if they so choose, to condemn.

It's deliberately and willfully making yourself vulnerable for something that you feel is bigger or more important than any one person—including yourself.

Everyone needs courage. Writers and creative geniuses are not exempt. And when they need it most is when they find courage in shortest supply. Oh, not for the big things. We all seem to muster the stuff for major crises. It's in the seemingly small incidents that we're forced to struggle to find so much as a seed or a grain of it.

That inability to summon it is pre-courage thinking and it's self-defeating, particularly for those intimately involved in creative endeavors, so...

Let's ditch it.

Common sense tells us that courage isn't something we have to seek. We all have it or we wouldn't have the guts to face every new day. We'd never have survived puberty. And we certainly never would have opened ourselves up to the criticisms and rejections we encounter as writers on a seemingly daily basis.

Common sense also verifies that those seemingly small incidents are the very ones that often alter our lives. For example, a writer submits a work twenty-one times and receives twenty-one rejection letters. But the writer doesn't lose faith in the work and she submits it again—and sells it. This *overnight success* took only the courage to make the twenty-second submission.

Or maybe a writer waffled on attending a conference. Maybe she heard a little voice inside her saying to go, but she just couldn't justify spending the money to attend the conference— it's a significant expense. But the little niggling voice persists, and so the writer listens to it and goes to the conference, anyway. And while there, she stumbles into an editor. They share a cup of coffee and connect on a project. And they're able to connect because the writer had the courage to listen to the little voice—her intuition.

Or perhaps the writer wrote a book, see-sawed back and forth on whether or not to include a risky secondary character, and did it. The public's response to that risky secondary character was so strong it warranted that character being awarded his own book. Because the writer had the courage to take the risk that intuitively she knew she needed to take.

These are small incident, yes, but ones with life-altering results. And each stemmed from the writer summoning just a bit of courage.

Now comes the root question.

> *Exactly how can you summon something*
> *inside you that you don't already have*
> *inside you?*

Fact is, you can't. But that isn't a challenge for courage. You might not know you have it. You might know you have it, and choose not to use it. Or, for any of a multitude of reasons, you might deny it exists. But the bottom line is that your belief has no impact on its existence, only on you. Courage is. It exists, and it is present inside you.

Courage existing being truth, we then must identify why we feel the need to seek it. If we seek what we've already got, then we're moving, but we can't be running toward anytⁱⁱⁱ. And if we're not running toward anything, and we're not standing still (no writer *ever* stands still), then we must be running away from something.

So what specifically are we running away from?

A likely candidate is our own fear and doubt. We fear condemnation, criticism, rejection. When confronted with any of the three, we doubt our judgment and ask ourselves if the thinking that led us to take this stand was really sound, solid and logical— or if it just seemed so at the time.

That we question ourselves proves we truly are not seeking courage, we're seeking respite. We want absolution from fear and doubt.

Doubt can be a demon, more potent than a plague, and it resides inside each of us. It rests comfortably, right there on the left shoulder of Fear. Like Fear, Doubt is relentless. Merciless. It attacks us when we least expect it—and when we're already down and we least need it.

Doubt makes us second-guess others' motives, the worthiness of all we do, and ourselves. The reasons are as varied as those that make us human. But three are particularly common:

1. **We fear reprisal, recrimination, losing an exalted status (or even an equitable one) in the eyes of others and in our own eyes.**

2. **We fear failure.**

3. **We fear success.**

Any of those three reasons can intimidate confident and balanced human beings to the point of completely stifling them. We harmony-seeking writers are particularly susceptible to all three.

We're busy, competitive people trying to do it all well, and we blanche and wither at the possibility of our professional or personal acumen not being *up to snuff*, at being considered inadequate, inept or ineffective. We want to represent ourselves well to others, confidently and standing on firm, sure-footed ground. We don't like criticism. We hate rejection. And we get more than our fair share of both. All writers do, regardless of their standing in the market.

Unfortunately, unless we work at attaining and maintaining a strong self-concept and sense of worth, we're going to have to do battle. Because criticism and rejection both feed the demon, Doubt.

When Doubt is well fed, it affects us enormously. We second-guess our decisions, our priorities, our personal values, and then we're vulnerable. From Doubt's left shoulder, Fear—who never misses a chance to feast on us when our defenses are down—lunches on our vulnerability. We worry about what kind of reception our new book will receive with our agent and/or publisher, in the marketplace, with reviewers, and we know that those receptions will affect us in our work and at home. Our families *do* know when the writing is going well, and when it is not. We reflect it in our mannerisms, with our attention, in our attitudes. We wear our moods.

Like in our works, in our professional and personal relationships, we open veins, letting bits and pieces of who we are, what we think, and how we feel seep through. We expose parts of our inner-selves to others. And we all want to shine.

It's human of us to want others to like those bits and pieces of us that we let them see. If they do, then we feel accepted and approved. Special and valued. It's our doubt that we will win acceptance and approval, that we will maintain our status or fail to achieve an aspired-to status that feeds our fear of failure. No one wants to fail. And to some degree, everyone fears it.

The more we fear failure, the more potent it becomes.

As its strength increases, so do its attacks on our self-esteem and the way we see ourselves. Because Fear's snacking on our sense of worth and that demon, Doubt, is sinking its talons into us, making mincemeat of our souls, we tend to forget that failure is proof of growth.

Someone wise once said, "If you're not failing, then you're not growing. If you're not growing, then you're standing still. And standing still, you're falling behind. You're just taking up space *and* losing ground.

That wise one was talking about the Universal Law of Momentum. Let's pause for a second and get a grip on it.

You start to move forward. You build a rhythm, a stride, and gain speed. But then you stop. When you stop you lose the rhythm, the stride and the speed. So you've lost ground because you aren't maintaining those things. But you've also lost the ground you would have covered by continuing without pause.

Think of the stone dropped in water. It causes a ripple. And as the ripple expands, it moves more water. The ripple just keeps broadening, impacting more and more water. That's momentum. Spreading. Growing. Expanding.

Common sense swears that it is no one's destiny to fall behind or to just take up space. And we should never fail to try because we fear failure. Fear and Doubt will do their damnedest to convince us that we should. They'll say we'll look like fools, that we'll be embarrassed... ashamed... sorry. But we have to be cold and objective and distance ourselves from Fear and Doubt to gain perspective. We also have to take an honest look at how we view failure and success.

Large chunks of concepts gag everyone. So let's break these fears down into bites that are easier for us to digest.

When we try something new and different, what are we actually doing?

We're making an attempt. Taking a stab at something. Making a trial run. We're writing a first draft. That's all. If we—our lives, or our works—were supposed to be perfect, wouldn't we skip the trial-and-error rituals and revisions and just leap straight to the success of the final draft?

When we make an attempt, even if we don't get where we wanted to go, or we don't accomplish exactly what we intended, we do move. Even when we write ourselves into corners and we must toss out all of the work done on a project and start over, we gain *something*. Some insight. Some sage wisdom. Something of value to us.

Well, gaining *something* is growth.

Growth is success.

And doesn't that prove that failure is a myth?

We forget these important things common sense tells us because Doubt, aided by Fear, encourages us to forget. Both of these demons are competent powerhouses when it comes to seeping inside us and then eating us alive. That means we must become competent powerhouses to overcome them as challenges and their influences on us. How do we do it?

By remembering this:

**Fear and Doubt only have as much
Power over us as we give them.**

We choose.

That's where courage comes in.

Having the courage to try something new is taking the first step. It's thumbing your nose at Fear and Doubt, which can make them double back and hammer you harder. But if you keep pushing and try anyway—in spite of them and their hammering— then you've already succeeded.

The secret is in recognizing that there is no failure.

Now, many of us fear success as much or even more than we fear failure. We want success. We struggle and sacrifice for it; crave it as much as we crave air and food. And yet when we achieve it—when we've reached that goal and have gotten that coveted agent to represent us, or we've sold that incredibly risky book to the exact editor at the exact publishing house we'd hoped to—then we fear our success and we doubt it.

I'm reminded here of a fabulously gifted author who had been underpaid for her novels for many years. She changed agents and this one got her six figures for her next novel. She phoned me, terrified. "I don't know how to write a hundred-thousand dollar book!"

But she'd been doing so for a long time. She finally had achieved the goal of being paid well, and now feared it. That fear crippled her in writing for nearly a year. But she stuck with it, and finally overcame it.

At times, we finally achieve success as we've defined it, and we actually sabotage it. We pause to emotionally react to the joy of achieving something we've worked hard to achieve, and then we turn on a dime and make ourselves nuts.

- *What if the agent doesn't like my next project?*

- *What if the editor leaves and I'm reassigned to a new editor who hates what I write?*

- *What if the book bombs in the market?*

- *No publisher in his right mind will risk ever publishing me again...*

Sound familiar?

Likely, it does. If it doesn't, ask about this in a group of writers and odds are high, you'll be the odd man out.

Rather than enjoying the victory, we wait for the other shoe to fall. For something or someone to snatch our success away. Or we doubt that whatever magic we possessed to pull off this success once was just a fluke—a one-time gift—and we'll never be able to conjure that magic or achieve that success again.

I'm going to tell on myself here. When I sold my first novel, I was hardly a newcomer to writing. I'd written fifteen books—with no concern whatsoever about where, how or if they'd fit into the market. Most of them didn't and they remain unsold. After six years of solid effort, and with all of these unsold novels collecting dust in my office closet on a shelf, I targeted a novel to a specific marketing niche and submitted it. I got *the call.* Finally, an editor wanted to buy my book.

I was thrilled—and doubtful. I was certain the editor had goofed. Positive that she'd meant to buy another writer's book and had gotten our manuscripts mixed up.

Rather than enjoying this hard-won moment, I lived in rigid fear that the error would be discovered. For two days, I refused to answer the phone. I did *not* want to receive that call, and I was convinced that the editor would be making it, telling me she was sorry, that the error had been made and discovered and she didn't want my book after all.

After two days, it occurred to me that if it had been an error, then surely it would have been discovered by now. But did I stop worrying? Uh, no. Instead of worrying that the editor had made a mistake in buying the book, I began worrying that I could never write another saleable book. After all, I had fifteen non-saleable books glaring at me, warming the office's closet shelf. The fear that I'd have to write fifteen more books before hitting on another one that was saleable wasn't totally out of the realm of reason...

But of course that fear *was* out of the realm of reason. In writing fifteen novels, I had learned a lot about writing and about writing commercial fiction. I couldn't go back to where I had been fifteen novels earlier. Why?

My experiences had changed me. Me, and my skills. My wheels, while not perfectly round, were less square than they had been back then.

My main point for relating this is to show you that I, too, was so busy fearing my success that I neglected to embrace the joy in achieving it. For me, the lesson was learned.

But unfortunately, in the years since that first sale, I've seen many other writers make the same mistake I made. Rather than enjoying the victory, they immediately began searching for the next hurdle.

Therein lies the tragedy.

We need to learn to appreciate the good times. To savor those glorious moment. They aren't rare, but neither are successes so plentiful that we should squander them.

There is a way to battle Doubt and Fear and win. As with any trial or tribulation, the first step in overcoming it is in recognition.

Realize that Doubt and Fear are normal, human responses that everyone feels. Accept that at some point in time both of them will show up in your life—professional and personal—and when they do, you'll have to battle them. Accept it.

And continue accepting it, knowing well that you might watch people you trained pass you up on the career ladder. Watch those people get better contracts, more lucrative offers. They could get more promotion perks, more attention from their agent and their editor and their publisher. They could enjoy higher sales, better reviews, more prestigious awards. It might even seem that they've made better marriages and built more content home lives. Acknowledge it all—including your awareness that Doubt and Fear can send you tumbling through a gauntlet of emotions that range from self-pity to rage.

Realize that during your writing life, some event *will* occur and leave you feeling as if you've hit bottom. Count on it. Possibilities?

∽ Your editor *will* leave or be promoted and you'll be culled from her list and reassigned to a new editor.

∽ The line you write for *will* fold, or the publisher will elect to cut the list and is no longer interested in acquiring your books.

∽ Your book will get a cover design that you feel is totally unsuitable for the book.

∽ An "Act of God" will occur and the train carrying all of your books to market will derail and the publisher will make a financial decision not to reprint it.

If only for a short time, you will decide that the personal costs of writing—particularly, the costs of writing for the commercial market—aren't worth the required sacrifices.

Realize that you will also experience times when you feel that you've worked harder for something you want than you've ever worked in your life—to get a risky novel published, to move up on the publisher's list, to gain credentials needed to provide a marketing hook in another type of writing—and you've failed to get it.

You *will* perceive this failure to achieve your goal not as a lack of your will or your personal effort, but as a personal lack in you. It isn't, of course, but nothing—nothing—will convince you of that.

The demon Doubt will work hard to make you believe all those things, and you will believe them—unless you consciously choose *not* to believe them.

Being aware and prepared for these curve balls Doubt and Fear are sure to sling at you, you're able to recognize them for what they are, and you'll be able to look the demons in the face and answer the cutting questions they hurl at you constructively. Questions like:

- *What if you don't sell that book?*

- *Negotiate a better contract?*

- *Make the bestseller list?*

- *What will people think?*

- *What will they say behind your back?*

- *They'll think you're a failure, a flop, a loser...*

- *And won't you be...?*

Common sense will intervene.

It'll tell you that it's what *you* think that matters. That if you don't sell the book or make the lists, then it's because you weren't meant to do so at this time. In some way, that gain would have been bad for you or it would have interfered with your personal growth or purpose. You might not understand why, or how getting what you want might be bad for you, but that's okay. Some things require courage—and a little faith.

That faith is an unshakable certainty that whatever happens to you, no matter how challenging, happens for your greater good. If you have the courage to embrace that belief and hold it close through good times and tough ones, then you can be at peace with the way things work out. Regardless of how they work out.

Ask yourself what value you place on specific goals, such as making the lists. Is that goal a realistic expectation? One you consider vital to you and your sense of value in the project?

Maybe you write category fiction but you feel inferior to those who write single-title novels. Maybe you love category-fiction writing and you have no desire to write anything else, and yet you feel you *should* write single-title novels because other people say you should. Whose opinions matter most? Your own, or those of others, who are walking different paths and looking at things through different perspectives—based on what they feel is most important to them?

If you are satisfied and content, isn't that enough? If it is not, then why is it not? If it is enough, then without apology or inferior feelings, accept it and embrace your contentment.

There is an enormous amount of power in acceptance. It gives you the freedom to stretch your comfort zone. Satisfaction and personal growth are but a few of its rewards. Doubt loses its stranglehold on you. And all you've really done is to face in your head what your heart has known all along: when you fight acceptance, you're at war with yourself. When you embrace acceptance, you find peace.

Fear will always rear its ugly head. And Doubt will always be riding shotgun on its left shoulder. But understanding and accepting both of these emotions as natural, normal human responses diminish either's ability to cut you as deeply as before you recognized and accepted them for what they are—and before you understood why they are as they are.

So what lessons have we learned from Doubt?

It can be a great teacher, if we open our minds and hearts to its lessons. They're simple ones; but then aren't the best (and most important) lessons *always* simple?

    Ș   Don't expect Doubt or Fear to ever totally cease. Both are perpetual, as much a part of life as breathing. What we allow to conjure Fear or Doubt in us changes faces, but Fear and Doubt remain.

෯ Don't deny or underestimate Fear or Doubt. Both are worthy adversaries (and at times, healthy friends). Acknowledge and accept them as part of what makes you human and respect their strengths. Recognize them for what they are—don't allow them to masquerade or trick you. In seeing Fear and Doubt as their true selves, you gain the power to find solutions that enable you not only to cope with them, but also to overcome many of their harmful pitfalls and negative effects.

෯ Don't allow criticism of your work to become a personal criticism that raises doubts about you, the person within. Your worth, your belief in yourself—those things are the essence of who you are, not what you do. And no one book can ever capture all the facets of you.

෯ Seek peace. Where you work or live is an outward expression of who you are. But either is only a facet of *all* you are. Everything that you do gives a more complete picture of you, the person. If you meet your eyes in the mirror and you like what you see, then you have succeeded in life and as a human being. If you don't like what you see, know that you have the power to change into a person that you do like and feel comfortable being. Neither Doubt nor Fear can compete with that kind of power.

෯ Remember: "Experience is not what happens to man. It is what man does with what happens to him." Aldous Huxley said it, and he was onto something special. We can't control the actions of others—our agents, our editors and publishers, reviewers or our readers. Nor can we control the actions of our spouses, kids, extended families, neighbors or our friends. We *can* control our reactions to their actions.

∽   Doubt can debilitate. It can chew you up and spit you out. It can also save your ass, so don't ignore its redeeming qualities. It can warn you against harm, against making mistakes that will adversely affect you—both short- and long-term. It can alert you *not* to take an easier path when the more difficult one will better serve you. The same duality holds true for Fear.

∽   Deny Doubt when it holds no value. Refuse to accept its claim in your life. Understand that peace isn't tied to what job you do, what car you drive, or what house you call home. Peace doesn't come from anything outside of you. Like security, peace comes from within.

You will always have doubts about something. You will always fear something. But because you've accepted Doubt and Fear and recognized that both can hold value, you've put them in their rightful places and discovered their true worth.

The difference in having done so is that your doubts are now about external affairs and not about the internal you. The you inside is no longer threatened by them. It's come to terms with the demons. In coming to terms, the demons have become your allies.

And now you know it isn't hard to have courage. We all have courage. We just had to get a grip and alter our perspective on Doubt and Fear.

Getting a grip. Mmm, that takes us to **Guidepost 2**.

ᦕ Guidepost 2 ᦥ

Getting a Grip

GOALS. OBJECTIVES. ASPIRATIONS. Keys to success.

By whatever name you choose to call these things, when you hone them down to bare-bones form, what you've got are concepts. I have a penchant for calling these concepts *Simple Truths* because they've proven themselves to be truths by appearing in my life, and in the lives of other writers around me, over and again.

Now some of these concepts we grasp quickly. There's nothing like being body-slammed to gain our attention, right?

But some of them are a little more subtle and more difficult for us to get a firm grip on. And still others grab us so hard that we swear they're jarring us half to death.

We're rolling along down the career road, working on rounding off our square wheels. But confronting the issues that round those square wheels alone daunts us. Overwhelms us. And, as I mentioned earlier, when we feel overwhelmed, we tend to avoid the issues we need to address rather than to take them on, break them down, and work past them.

Getting a grip on these concepts isn't as hard as we might think. But we've got to take the plunge, wade through the puddles, and risk squishing a little mud between our toes to do it. Sometimes, a lot of mud.

One of our greatest assets is in realizing that we are not alone. Other writers share our experiences and our challenges.

For example, after I sold my first book, my editor was promoted. While thrilled for her, I was understandably anxious for me. The book was not yet on the shelves in stores, and I, through no action of my own, crossed the ranks to the one-book, orphaned author. My old editor had read and loved a proposal I'd prepared for a second book and, while she would have purchased it on a proposal, she felt my new editor, who needed time to get settled into her new job, might prefer to have the book finished before buying it. Truthfully, I wasn't enamored with the idea of writing a complete book without a contract. But I figured I was going to write it anyway, and my old editor had been so enthusiastic about the proposal, so... why not? I finished the book and then submitted it to my new editor.

Now the editor who had acquired my first book and I were on the same wavelength. We both liked suspense and dark-toned novels. Gripping stories. As this book was targeted for a line that contained suspenseful, dramatic elements, I thought everything would be fine.

As it turned out, things were not fine.

The differences in editorial tastes were significant. The new editor phoned, saying that she'd read the book and it had given her nightmares for a week. Considering that I'd written a dark, suspenseful, dramatic book for a line with those qualities, I interpreted her comments as high praise. It was not. She preferred "simple stories" that were "lighter in tone" and that had "less complex plots."

I was sunk. Inside, I knew it. We were a bad match, and there was no way around it. But I fought it. For the next eighteen months, I sincerely and diligently tried to write a novel that the new editor would like. I never did. My confidence in my ability to write took a serious nose-dive. My belief in my ability to handle the projects I was taking on faded. Finally, a light bulb went on in my mind. Hell, if what I was writing was being rejected *anyway*, then I might as well collect rejections on novels *I* loved and wanted to write—and just what made this one editor "all knowing" on my work; so all knowing I gave her all the power on deciding my future? Had I lost my mind, doing that?

Well, I didn't admit I'd lost my mind, but I did admit I'd suffered a serious, serious judgment lapse. So I nixed it. Took back control and reclaimed my personal power to drive my own career boat.

That day, I stopped deliberately trying to write to please an editor—*any* editor. I stopped writing someone else's stories, and returned to writing my own. I set a policy. I wouldn't close my mind to constructive criticism, but I would remember that any criticism was that person's opinion, not law. I'd write my books my way, and take my hits or kudos for them with dignity and grace. Most importantly—and this is the major big point—I made myself a promise that I will keep until the day I die with a pencil in my hand: *I will only write stories I love.*

I sold four novels within the next six months.

Now, eighteen months of writing and never completing a novel is a tough stretch for a writer—no payoff for all the work. That's particularly tough on a newly published writer who hasn't yet experienced much positive reinforcement on her writing abilities.

During those dark times, I grew more and more morose, and even more convinced that selling the first book and the editor loving the partial on the second book had been a fluke. Obviously, I couldn't write. How dare I even call myself a writer?

Things got bad. Really bad.

Then, they got worse.

Or did they?

With the clarity of hindsight, I can tell you that what happened was a blessing in disguise. Let's look at the scenarios.

If during those eighteen months, the new editor had bought the license on the novels I proposed, I would have written them. And as long as she kept buying, I would have kept on writing them. It can take a very long time to reverse the effects of writing fifteen novels and waiting for six years for that first sale.

But she didn't buy them, and for that, I owe her a debt of gratitude I can never repay. In essence, she forced me to get a grip and re-evaluate. I had to consciously decide whether to keep trying to please her, or to starting trying to please me by writing the books I *really* wanted to write.

While I might well have earned a good living, I doubt I would have felt the same sense of satisfaction I feel at writing only books I love so much that I can't not write them. That personal investment of emotion, dedication, and faith in a work is the

Vicki Hinze

magic in novels. It makes a difference, and that difference shows in the work.

So was this dark time a bad thing? It felt like it at the time, and some might perceive it as such still. But having been the one who experienced it, I can tell you with total conviction that it was clearly a good thing. If not pushed, we seldom upset the status quo and grow—even when it's what we really want, and what we initially set out to do.

We're human. And humans learn most effectively from experience. But there's no law that says every experience must be learned firsthand. We don't have to trudge through every single mud puddle or roll over every bump on the career road and hit every single pothole to know that it's muddy or rocky or has bumps and potholes. We can learn from others' experiences *if* we give ourselves permission to learn from them. By doing so, we can avoid hitting the bumps and holes and mud puddles that they've hit. We will hit others, and perhaps others can learn from them and the experience pool will broaden and deepen and be easier on all of us. I know of no writer who wouldn't have a genuine appreciation for that!

So what specifically are these concepts, and how can they help us identify who we are and what we want to claim as parts of our lives? How can these concepts offer us insights into ways we can simplify our thinking, ditch some of our stress, and find the balance and inner peace, which is so integral to our writing and our quality of life?

In getting a grip, we recognize that the two are intertwined.

Let's look at the concepts singularly, beginning with being flexible—**Guidepost 3**.

ᡃᡃGuidepost 3 ᠀

Flexible

BY CHOICE OR NECESSITY, successful writers who are balanced and at peace with themselves are flexible.

And it's a good thing, because our industry is one of the most dynamic in existence—and if we're lucky, it always will be.

As people, we constantly change, which means our writing constantly changes. Our industry too must change to reflect the changes in us as people.

Change of any kind can be intimidating, and it's often difficult. But it is necessary. Because to not change is to stay the same—to become stagnant. Stagnant people develop problems like depression, apathy, and anxiety attacks. Some scientific research indicates there's a correlation between a lack of stimuli and diseases like Alzheimer's. And what happens to stagnant industries?

They die.

Translated into book-talk, what exactly does being flexible mean?

On a personal level, it means writers must have the courage to be open to new discoveries and ideas, to new methods and ways of doing things. Being flexible is exhibiting a willingness to blend the old ways with the new. And new ways, provided we welcome them, can still be uncomfortable but also exciting, interesting, intriguing.

We get a grip when we welcome the opportunity to be flexible in mind, body and spirit. When we see value and the potential for finding balance and harmony that comes to us when all of the parts of us work together cohesively, as a unit.

How do we translate that into concrete action in our writing lives?

- By adopting a "Yes, I'll try that" attitude.

- By being eager to explore.

- By reading not only information we must read for the novels we're currently writing, but other information, too.

- By reading not only works that interest us, or ones that mirror our own opinions, but material and works with opposing opinions.

- By honing our observation skills.

- By listening *and* hearing what others saying to us in conversations with them.

- By writing something new and different. Something we expect to like *and* something we aren't sure we'll like.

- By giving ourselves permission to explore and experiment.

- By keeping an open mind and looking for the best, not the worst—in our works, and in other people.

Being flexible is looking outside yourself and your preferences, beyond biased notions and prejudices, presumptions and predispositions. It's seeing something specific from another person's perspective, through another person's eyes. It's respecting another person even when you disagree with his or her opinions, ideas, or views.

Being flexible is also accepting that others will disagree with you, and that's fine. It is also accepting that you don't always have to be right, the center of attention, or the boss. Even if you're a natural-born leader, you can learn a great deal from following.

I'm not saying you should allow yourself to become shoe dirt on someone else's stomping grounds. Or that you should bend so much that you break.

I'm saying that there is value in trying new things, in seeing the worthiness in other people's ideas, and in the way that they accomplish both similar and dissimilar tasks.

Rigidity isn't an asset if it blocks your ability to see the good in other people or in new-to-you methods. It's a liability. Don't intentionally become its victim. Why cut off your nose (and yourself) to spite your face (and your creativity)?

At a conference once, a writer boldly and loudly insisted that she would never revise a book. It didn't matter to her that the book might well benefit from revisions, which is often the case. She would *not* revise—*ever.*

For some reason known only to God and her, this writer exempted herself from the "being too close to the forest to see the trees" syndrome that every other writer suffers. Everyone in the group made an attempt to offer this writer a wiser perspective and the insight to make better choices on the topic of revisions, but her mind was sealed tighter than a tarred drum. Her books were hers, and any requested revisions that she agreed to do would be an artistic compromise and an insult to her talent.

Strong opinions, indeed, but I ask you, how can a willingness to revise to make a novel stronger be considered an artistic insult? Isn't it a greater insult to close your mind to educated suggestions to enhance your work? In refusing to even consider recommendations, isn't it entirely possible that the writer is denying the novel an opportunity to realize its full potential?

Sadly, I believe it is and the writer has condemned herself and her work to learning this School of Hard Knocks lesson.

An open mind is a wonderful thing, and yet there will be times when two professionals—the writer and the editor—do disagree. It's at that point when both professionals exercise an extremely powerful option. It's called compromise. And all relationships, professional and personal, benefit from a steady diet of it.

It takes two people to argue. One person can't argue alone. Disagreements are inevitable, especially when dealing with something as subjective as writing a book. But both professionals always hold a powerful option to diffuse tension:

At any time, either party can simply agree to disagree.

That modest statement expresses genuine respect for the other person's opinions and for your own. You're not trying to strong-arm anyone into thinking your way or into changing his mind. You're accepting that, on this issue, you disagree. And that gives you both latitude—without defensive baggage intruding—to look for solutions that both professionals consider agreeable. Solutions where everyone wins.

That's the key to terrific solutions. There are no losers. And there is an uncomplicated win/win-solution technique that is as effective as it is simple:

**Approach problems, challenges or trials,
determined to resolve them in good faith.**

No one is all wrong or all right. Diversity is an asset. Respect similarities *and* differences. Sometimes, you'll meet halfway. Sometimes you'll take an extra step or two, or twenty. Sometimes the other party will. The end result is what most matters, not who took what steps or how many steps they took. Remember that: *The end result.*

A side effect of being flexible and willing to compromise is that you build trust and develop a reputation for being fair.

That often results in other people being more willing to compromise. If you, a fair person, consider a request reasonable, then it must hold merit.

What happened to the author who refused to consider revisions?

She developed a reputation in the industry as an author who "is difficult to work with"—which in all fairness, she was—

and she couldn't sell her work. I'm not sure if she's still writing now, but we can all learn from her experience.

No writer should be a doormat—that's destructive to self-respect—but all writers should be open-minded and willing to listen to others' ideas and views and opinions, and willing to acknowledge that whether or not we agree, those ideas, views, and opinions hold merit.

I'm a firm believer in helping others. Doing so feeds the soul, and the simple truth is that all of our souls are hungry. At times, they're starved. Helping someone else forces us to look beyond ourselves, our situations, our lives, and to really see others, their situations and lives and their struggles. Doing "good" makes us feel good, as if we're making a difference. And in reaching out, we are.

So what if you would like to reach out to others, but you're so overtaxed now that you just can't take on one more thing—and then you're asked to take on one more thing?

This situation frequently occurs in the life of a writer. You'll get a phone call or an email, asking you to come do a workshop, to judge a writing competition, to critique an entire manuscript, to endorse a book, or to act as a mentor for a writing group. This new task will require time you don't have to spare. *But it's such a worthy cause*, the writer thinks. *If I get up an hour earlier for two weeks, that extra time should cover the work requested, and I still should be able to meet my scheduled deadlines on everything else...*

The writer is so tempted to defy common sense and take on the task, anyway.

But the writer must be disciplined—and she must do everyone involved a favor:

Listen to common sense and say no.
Without guilt.

If you're doing all you can, then that's all you can do. Don't feel you must justify your reasoning or your rationale.

No *is* a complete sentence.

Don't feel badly. You know your limit, know you are already doing as much as you can do. And you know that when you've reached your limit, putting one more thing on your plate is self-destructive.

Denying your human limitations is destructive.

Committing to do something and then not doing your best to complete the act is destructive, too.

When we must refuse someone something, naturally we don't feel good about it. As harmony-seeking writers with strong memories of how desperately we needed help as new writers, we want to honor our instinctive reaction, to be gracious and say yes to requests as often as possible. That's because writers are creative, caring, loving people who genuinely want to help—and they should. But they should do so judiciously and realistically.

They have a responsibility to accept that there are times when they can assist, and there are times when assisting just isn't possible. And if we deny logic and take on the task anyway, then we've created real problems. Problems for ourselves, and for those we intended to help.

We feel guilty, or we fear that not helping those who ask will have an adverse affect on our relationships or even our careers. (Have you ever been asked by the boss to plan the company picnic—on your own time?)

In some situations, we feel compelled to agree rather than to refuse. We resent it. We're angered by it. But we still do it. Why?

We fear failure.

And we fear success.

Which brings us to **Guidepost 4.**

⚒Guidepost 4 ⚒

Fear of Success

WE'VE TOUCHED ON THIS TOPIC PREVIOUSLY, but the fear of success, like Fear and Doubt, is a worthy adversary that we must deal with decisively in order to put balance back into our lives and find inner peace. When tormented within, what writer can focus intently on a novel?

As human beings, we focus on whatever is troubling us. We don't think deeply about our newest plot, the dimensions of our characters, or how tightly our novel elements are interwoven. We focus on our troubles.

We must accept that human limitation, pause, and deal with the issue troubling us in a positive, constructive manner. At ease personally, we are then free to give our work the attention it deserves.

Though not discussed as openly or with the same vigor as the fear of failure, the fear of success is common to human beings. In cases, that fear is deep-seated in others, it hovers just beneath our surfaces. To some of us, that fear is an asset. It encourages us to do our best. For others, the fear stifles them and inhibits growth. The lack of growth in a writer is stagnation, and we've already covered what happens when anything stagnates. Writers aren't exempt.

How strong a punch the fear of success packs depends on the person battling it. If you're in a safe, tame and familiar career, then odds are that the fear isn't as powerful a force in your life than if you're in a career that requires you to take a substantial number of risks.

All creative people are continually called upon to take risks.

Most writers share this human fear to some extent and yet its power over them is a little different than it is for non-writers. Think about it. If writers allowed the odds of success to daunt them, wouldn't they choose safer, tamer careers? Wouldn't they be space explorers, snake charmers, or bomb-squad specialists?

Instead, writers do the really dangerous stuff. They slice open veins, pour out their souls in books that they then offer to the world to judge.

While this fear is different for writers, few are exempt from experiencing it. For us, often this fear just changes faces. When you're a new writer, the fear of success translates to a fierce need to get something you've written published. Publication is affirmation that you can write. Walk into any group, and as soon as someone asks what you do and you answer that you're a writer, the next question you'll hear is:

What have you published?

Many, many fine writers are not published. Some extremely skilled writers are not published. Some, for reasons of their own, never seek, try, or attempt to get published—and if it were offered to them, they would refuse it. Some fine writers seek publication and run into brick walls. And then more brick walls. Perhaps the writer's work is excellent, just not commercial. Or perhaps the writer pushed the boundaries a little to far to fit into a currently defined marketing niche. Or perhaps a work lacks a marketing hook.

It often happens that quality work isn't publishable for reasons that have absolutely nothing to do with the work but with marketing. Or various other reasons, including similarity with a work already purchased. And yet the writer is judged and validated by others based solely on the virtue of publication.

This mind-set stems from one of society's widely accepted labels. Your personal and professional worth are judged by the amount of money you make. For the writer, it's the same ideal or concept; it's just wearing a different face. An unpublished writer often *and* erroneously isn't considered to be a "serious" writer until he or she publishes a work. As writers who help other writers, we all know that this standard isn't a fair gauge, but we also know that it takes time, effort and energy to change society's views. For now, we must be content knowing that we're working on it.

Now, the writer struggles, sacrifices, and finally gets a novel published. Is the writer pleased?

Yes. But Fear and Doubt, doing what they do best, attempt to steal the joy and the thunder. They intrude, filling the newly published writer's head with doubts that lead the fragile writer, who is already walking on unfamiliar ground and into the unknown, to ask questions like:

- *Can I sell another novel, or am I a one-book wonder?*

- *Did the editor make a mistake? Maybe she did. Maybe she will call back and say, "Sorry. I meant to reject your novel. It's drivel. I thought it was another writer's book..."*

But the purchase wasn't a mistake, and time passes, putting those fears to rest. The writer is now multi-published and has several books on store shelves. Does that fear cut the writer any slack now, so that she can enjoy this success?

Yes, and no.

More often than not, this joy too is waylaid by visits from Fear and Doubt, who pose even more tormenting questions to the writer. Questions like:

- *Can you really continue to write better books?*

- *Can you maintain or exceed the quality of the work with each successive book?*

- *Haven't you done your best work already? From here on out, you're doomed to a downhill slide— it's inescapable!*

The point I'm making is that regardless of what stage of the writing career a writer is in, she is constantly faced with new challenges. Bombarded with new fears and uncertainties that must be faced. As soon as one challenge is met and mastered, another jumps in to take its place. Always, another takes its place. *Always.*

Know it. Be prepared for it. And allow your common sense to remind you that joy is *not* arriving at a destination. It's in taking the ride.

We're writers. We're not kids in the backseat on a car trip with the folks, shouting, "Are we there yet?" We're on a bigger trip. Ultimately, our destination is the end of life as we know it. There, we discard the shell and our spirits go on to a new journey, but *this* journey is over.

Joy is found in appreciating the good *during* this journey, *throughout* our careers and our lives. It's found in feeling re-warded by the good we do, the lives we touch, the worthy things we accomplish and the caring we express along the way.

As you progress in your writing career, understand that new challenges are new opportunities for growth. To round the square wheels here (or to ditch them), you must dig deeply into your most secret self and recognize that denying yourself the op-portunity to grow is rooted in fear. Expose the fear for what it is. Look at it coldly and objectively. And then grab hold of your backbone and face those opportunities the only way that you can successfully face anything: with your own inner courage.

I don't know if you believe in God, a Deity, or a Higher Power, but if you, then you have a mind-set available to you that gives you an immense amount of leverage in battling this fear. It is:

God doesn't make trash. Nor does He challenge wimps. And He never gives one the desire to do something without also giving them the talent to make that desire manifest.

Simple truths, one and all. Proven facts. And evidence that even when you doubt it, you *can* handle whatever happens to you at any given time in your life or whatever is happening, would *not* be happening to you.

I'll admit that there have been times in my career and in my life when I've wondered if maybe God hadn't set a heavy challenge on my shoulders and then dozed off for an afternoon nap. But in retrospect, and with the clarity of hindsight, I've learned that what I gained from the challenging experience was something I needed to know. Something that helped me deal constructively with other things in future events.

What I had perceived as bad proved to be good. (Remember the dark time? That eighteen months of writing proposal after proposal without even the satisfaction of finishing a book?) That experience and all the lessons learned there prepared me for some important, future life events and equipped me to deal with those events in a positive manner. I'd have been lost without that experience—and likely would have failed to reach major objectives that, because I was prepared, I did reach.

The insight that I'm now going to suggest likely directly contrasts with what you've been told by others. You've heard repeatedly that no one is indispensable.

The simple truth is that *all* of us are indispensable, and not one of us—*not one*—is expendable.

We're all unique in our own way, and the world is different because each of us is in it. No other writer could write our same book. *Ever.* We have no exact duplicate, and we do have the tools necessary to manifest our gifts.

Thomas J. Watson so eloquently and wisely reminded us that the "simple formula for achieving success is to double your failure rate."

Therein lies your license to fail.

Guilt-free.

Whether we're discussing writing or life, we now realize that the fear of success is a double-edge sword. We desperately want success and fear achieving it, and we fear that if we do achieve it, we won't be able to maintain it.

I personally can't fathom anyone trying something new and not learning *something* from the experience. I've had my fair share of opportunities to draw that conclusion, but when the balance sheet reconciles, I've consistently found that, whether or not the attempted goal was attained, *something* was gained. Be it a new skill, an insight into some sage wisdom I lacked before the experience, or a new understanding that increased business savvy. Always, I gained something worth the effort.

This logic works for me in writing, because I can't imagine any author writing an entire novel and learning nothing. I just can't imagine it. Like ninety-nine percent of all other writers, I've gotten tons of rejection letters—enough to wallpaper the White House. But I can't say that I've ever written a novel and not learned something in doing it.

One very valuable lesson I've learned is that rejection letters are worth five minutes of foot-stomping, hell-raising, and questioning of the editor's parentage or sense. But no rejection letter is worth one second more of upset. Not one second more.

I learned this valuable lesson from Susan, a writer further up the career ladder, who was gracious enough to share her insights. In a group of writers, I overheard Susan say to a third writer, "A rejection letter is simply an invitation to submit elsewhere."

I liked that! Rather than feeling the negativity of rejection, I felt the positive influence of an invitation. Nothing had changed except my perspective.

Often, rejection letters are not a reflection of the work, but of the market at that time, or of the publisher's current list.

For example. You've written a medieval novel set in Scotland. The editor loves your novel, but she's just bought two other novels set in medieval Scotland. She can't buy a third or it'll upset the balance of her list. So your novel is rejected. But this rejection has nothing to do with your work, or with the quality of it.

Frequently, the problem we have with reconciling our gains or losses is our perception—the way we choose to look at an experience. Our own mind-set. Embracing a positive mind-set is a key to success.

When we duck into denial, we get into trouble. We must acknowledge that we are worthy of success. And we must give ourselves permission to fail our way to it.

This permission doesn't take as much courage as we once thought, because we've already learned that failure is growth, growth is success, and—whether or not we reach our intended goal—we've gained something—therefore, failure is a myth.

By acknowledging that you are worthy of success and giving yourself permission to not be perfect—it's okay not to achieve your initial goal every time—you liberate yourself from your uncertainties. If you're adept at this, then you might just fumble and stumble and fail your way to genius!

Of course, a writer's odds are greatly enhanced if she develops thick skin.

If you doubt you need it, are uncertain you want it, or you're not quite sure what developing a thick skin means in real terms, read on to **Guidepost 5**.

⇜Guidepost 5 ⇝

Develop Thick Skin

LET'S BE CLEAR. I'm not giving any writer a license to become an insufferable twit or an insensitive jerk. I am recommending that every writer recognize the result of *not* developing the kind of thick skin I'm referencing. And that is developing ulcers, depression, anxiety, and worse.

Let me share an example with you.

I have a good friend who is also a writer named Phyllis. For many years, Phyllis read everything I wrote—and she bled all over it. I swore that no one pen could hold that much red ink. Once, I told Phyllis that my goal was for her to critique my work and send it back to me "bloodless."

A few days later, I received a postcard in the mail from her. On it, Phyllis had written:

It takes a lot of heat to temper steel.

Phyllis was right. Regardless of what work you do, or what goal you're aspiring to meet, you can't expect to walk into it and be good at it without first investing in it. No matter how much you love whatever you're going after, it is difficult and challenging, and you've got to pay your dues. That's not good news for those who are mired in a world that demands instant gratification, but it is a fact, nonetheless.

Like tempering steel, tempering the writer—developing voice, style; finding that perfect niche—takes time, effort and discipline. You have to have the courage to invest in yourself—and you will, if you want something badly enough.

I'm sorry to say that I've forgotten who said this—(though honesty demands it, that's a terrible admission for an author to have to make)—but it is appropriate. "You can't have everything you want. You can have the things you want most."

Do you know what you want most? If so, great. Go for it. If not, it's time to sit down and have a deep and serious, heart-to-heart talk with yourself to find out what you most want and then form a concrete plan of action for pursuing it.

So often I see writers crushed by criticism, by critique partners and contest judges who scored their work low, by unthinking spouses, by editors who unfortunately must say no far more often than they get to say yes. The key here is to realize that developing thick skin insulates the writer. It gives the writer a little space, a little distance and objectivity, so the writer can see that professional criticisms and/or rejections are directed at the work and not at the writer.

Another area in which the writer needs thick skin is in being persistent in the pursuit of the writing life *he* or *she* truly wants. Not the writing life a significant other, spouse, parent, or anyone else wants for the writer—no matter how well meaning. But the writing life the writer wants.

On occasion, a writer does receive a criticism or rejection that is directed at the writer personally. What do you do then?

You remember what common sense tells you. You can't control anyone else's actions; only your own. But you most definitely can control your reactions to others' actions. You decide how deeply you let the opinions of others affect you. You determine how much power you give that person and their criticism over you and your life that day. Remember, other people are human, too, and humans have hot buttons. So whether or not you consider the criticism valid, say, "Thank you. I appreciate your opinion and I'll give it serious consideration."

That's it.

I know, you'd love to raise a ruckus, ask who the spit she thinks she is, and spew all sorts of snappy comebacks. Don't.

When bitten, the human reaction is to bite back. But in biting back, you validate the other person's negative opinion.

You feed it your energy. Do you really want to do that? Doesn't common sense tell you that you would be wiser and stronger and exhibit more character by diffusing the situation of tension, by retaining reason and dignity?

Another oh-so-human reaction to criticism is to defend yourself and/or your work. But again, if you do, you're accomplishing nothing, only feeding it your energy. Better to drain its strength and end the discussion before harsh words are spoken and relationships are damaged.

This does *not* mean that you take a hit for something that isn't your fault, or that you tolerate verbal abuse. Those things you nix—*now*. Calmly. It's most often little digs which get us into trouble, either through intent or through perceived intent.

An important point to remember:

It takes two people to sustain a conflict.

One can't do it alone. You choose whether or not to engage and participate—and whether or not to continue to engage and/or participate.

Now, let's pause for a moment and put the shoe on the other foot. How often do you find fault with others? With yourself? Do you feel compelled to *always* correct others, privately or publicly?

If not, then good for you. You don't have to worry about someone coming along and holding you up to your own tandards. And overlooking a few flaws in others is a healthy thing.

If you are critical, then work to stop it. We're all works-in-progress. Okay, so some of us do need *more* work and progress than others. But *none* of us are perfect.

This is a glorious discovery because, from our fiction writing, we know that perfect in novels is boring, and boring is deadly. Thankfully, none of us humans have that problem. But being on the receiving end of criticism, especially constant criticism (read that *nagged),* makes us edgy and unhappy. It alienates us, and it builds tons of resentment. We avoid people who make us feel badly about ourselves, and all that criticism doesn't do a damn thing that is positive. It doesn't encourage us to change anything or to alter our attitudes in our ways. It does encourage us to shut down and back away. It's destructive, and it tramples feelings and irritates. These are not personal attributes that we typically admire in other people. So why deliberately encourage them in others—or in ourselves?

The exception to this is *constructive* criticism. When offered diplomatically and discreetly, it can be very helpful. But constructive criticism is never harsh or biting. It's given in good faith to help or assist the receiver. It acknowledges an understanding of the blood, sweat and sacrifices the writer has made and all s/he has poured into the work. And common sense warns us that if we have a choice, like with advice, we should refrain from giving our opinion unless it is solicited or we note signs that our views would be welcome.

What if you're in a critique group meeting and you believe a member could benefit from your constructive criticism? Should you wait to approach her?

If possible, work with that person until s/he is in a receptive frame of mind, and then share not only the constructive criticism of their work but also the positive attributes in it that you've noted. We need to know what we've done that works well just as much as we need to know what isn't working well. Weigh the writer's reaction, her body language. Some writers are receptive and have a good attitude, appreciate comments. Some haven't yet evolved to that point and just want praise. You don't know which a writer is until you investigate a bit. Either way, I suggest you exercise caution.

Offering great advice with the best of intentions can still be unwelcome or unwanted. And no writer ever wants to feel that s/he's crushed another writer's creative hope. For the more fragile among us, the effects of something like that can be far-reaching and long lasting.

The reason why you must exercise such caution, beyond all the obvious reasons, is that regardless of how well you critique and how insightful you are, your opinion is subjective and only your opinion. Another writer, one who is equally gifted at rendering critical opinions and insights, well might respond differently to the work. There are no absolutes in writing, and it would be unacceptable to devastate someone on the false premise that there are absolutes.

Remember, too—it bears repeating—that knowing what we're doing right or well in our work is just as important as knowing what we're doing that could benefit from improvement.

In that respect, writers can learn a great deal from skilled editors' revision letters. The best of these letters open with over-all comments that focus on what is working well in the project submitted. Then the editor discloses areas that could benefit from revisions. The letter closes with a recap of all that is right and working well.

The old adage of the spoonful of sugar helping the medicine go down is evident in the structure of these revision letters. The writers who critique for others, or judge them in writing competitions and note comments on the work, would stand themselves in good stead to learn from these editorial treasures.

Another situation in which thick skin proves its worth is when someone wants something for you that is different from what you want for yourself. It could be a parent who wants you to attend college at their alma mater, to follow in their career footsteps, or an editor or a spouse who recommends a career path or move that isn't consistent with one you want to make. When you get down to the bottom line, they're one in the same: someone else making your choices for you for reasons of their own that might or might not be what they feel is best for you.

It might be advantageous to an editor for you to take a specific path. To a spouse. For example:

Let's say you're writing three category novels per year. You do so consistently and your sales are good. You wish to write a single title novel, but the editor advises that it's a better career move for you to stay with the category novel. Well, it could be that it is. But it could also be that these slots are not that easily filled well, and you do so. And that the editor knows she can count on you to do so with books that sell. That impacts the editor's bottom line and that governs her promotions and bonuses.

Remember, it isn't a matter of the editor being "mean" or insincere. It is the editor's job to do what is best for her company. That *is* her job and her primary responsibility. You shouldn't resent an editor for doing her best to fulfill her responsibilities. She has hers and you have yours.

Doing your best for you is your responsibility.

A spouse might well advise against writing that single title because the income on those three categories each year is consistent and steady, and there is no guarantee that the single title will earn the same or better. It could earn less. So the spouse may genuinely feel it is in your best interest to stick with the category novels because the view is it is a known quantity and that makes it in your best financial interest.

But there are other interests to consider, and only you can define what they are and how important they are to you. So while you might solicit the opinions of others, make your own decisions, and if a suggested career move isn't one you want to make, then don't.

Some will attempt to use guilt to "encourage" you to go against your own wishes, anyway. Don't let it. If you do, regret and resentment *will* fester inside you and destroy whatever shot you've got for inner peace or contentment. It will also carry over into the relationship with whoever is doing that parsing using guilt. I won't say it's easy to refuse; it's not. You respect your editor and love your spouse and that makes going against them difficult. These people have been supportive, likely good to you—maybe believed in you when you weren't sure you believed in yourself.

But you must call upon your courage and inner knowing of what the end result will be with that resentment and be persistent in pursuing the life you most want to live. The path that you most want to take—or not take. Because in the end, it will be you, and you alone, who looks back and lives forever with your actions.

And it will be you, not the editor and not your spouse, who lives with the discontent and with the regret of what you did and did not do. For that reason, your path should be your choice.

What about judging others? Do you make certain assumptions about a person based solely on appearance?

Of course, you do. We all do. But common sense requires more from us than an exterior, visual scan to assess a person's worth. If we could choose, we would all be gorgeous, wealthy, whole. Well, some of us would.

Those who don't understand the concept of trials (whether emotional, spiritual, or physical) being tools to foster personal growth, being a means of building character and defining personal philosophy. When things are going great, we don't gain much as human beings. It's through the tough times that we come to know ourselves, to determine what we think and feel and the type of people we are and we want to be.

We all know better than to judge a book by its cover. Why don't we extend that same courtesy to people?

Complicated question, but it has a simple answer.

Because we choose not to extend it. This choice is representative of our mind-set, and it's a breeding ground for conflict. That isn't conducive to our attaining balance and harmony in our lives. So what is?

Altering that mind-set to one that better serves us as people. Whatever better serves us as people better serves our work and our ability to perform it. That takes us to **Guidepost 6.**

✒Guidepost 6 ✒

Mind-set

IN MY HUMBLE, IF NOT UNBIASED OPINION, writers are amazing people. Their gifts of making something real out of nothing are so ordinary to them that often they forget how extraordinary this gift makes them.

True, much of writing can be learned. But there is a fabulous spark that is a gift. It's that spark that fosters storytelling that touches hearts, offers different perspectives, and changes attitudes.

Attitude *is* mind-set. And mind-set is, simply put, a matter of choice.

You decide whether the proverbial cup is half-empty or half-full. The choices you make are a reflection of the person you are. The person you choose to be. And the person you choose to be goes a long way toward defining the novels you write.

From birth, we are molded and shaped to think and feel certain ways about specific things and about things in general. A lot of factors help determine this molding into who we are and what kind of people we become: our background, history, the nature and quality of our family life. The views of those closest to us, of those we love and respect. Cause and effect experiences we encounter. Our traumas and crises, our awards and honors. Positive and negative experiences encountered impact us—even the strangers we meet by chance.

Inside, we're a bowl of soup, a unique and exotic blend of all we've learned, experienced, dreamed and desired, feared and hated, loved and embraced. But where we choose to place emphasis and focus—that's up to us.

A couple of years ago, I heard a saying. (If you haven't yet gathered it on your own, I collect sayings that touch me deeply.) Though I've no idea who wrote this one, it ricocheted off my ribs and claimed an entire chamber of my heart.

> *Our deepest fear is not that we are inadequate.*
> *Our deepest fear is that we are powerful beyond*
> *measure. It is our light, not our darkness, that*
> *most frightens us. We ask ourselves, Who am I*
> *to be brilliant, gorgeous, talented, fabulous?*
> *Actually, who are you not to be?*

If you have any sense of worth at all, that saying is sheer TNT.

So often, writers view themselves only as the person who sits at the kitchen table with pen and pad, or at the computer keyboard, who dreams and then breathes life into that dream through the written word. While that is true and part of what writers are, it's not all of who they are, or all of what they do. Writers are more. Far more. And it's up to them to unearth all that it is their destiny to be, and then to become it.

We all do have worth. We all are given sparks of genius. Regardless of our position, standing or financial status, we all have the potential to touch lives, to open doors in minds that were previously closed. To make a difference.

Yet another mind-set challenge is in seeing ourselves only as an extension of someone else. Women are particularly vulnerable to this. *I'm so-and-so's wife, mother, daughter, sister.* But men are not exempt. They go through these extension identity crises, too.

As writers, we study human nature and explore it in our novels. We work to hone our observation skills, to home in on the gems that hide under all the window-dressing and pomp and circumstance, and in doing so, we really sympathize with men today—especially in their interactions with women. Even the tiniest actions can cause them an enormous amount of anxiety.

For example. A man and woman meet at the door to a shop. Does the man open the door for the woman, or not? The best the guy can hope for is fifty-fifty odds. For his trouble, he could be thanked or thwapped.

It's interesting to watch men in these types of simple situations. It's painful, too, seeing their discomfort. They size up the woman, trying to decide what to do, often vacillating between doing nothing and doing something. Risky business, they know, certain they'll either be considered enlightened or damned rude. Given a choice, of course they would prefer to be considered enlightened. But how can they tell if they're eye-balling an advocate of door-opening or a woman who will take strong and serious exception to the gesture that once was considered simply courteous and polite—a sign of respect?

Guys are in a real pickle on these type things. I vote that we cut them a little slack. If one opens a door, fine. If not, then that's fine, too. Either way, we women should smile and thank them. They'll feel better and we'll feel better, knowing we helped them ditch some useless and unproductive anxiety.

Of course, the guy will probably wonder if the smile is sincere or sarcastic, but we can't cure all ails at once. We're only human, so we'll do what we can, and offer him a kind word, too.

And we'll think about this whole door-opening episode. About all of this politically correct business. I mean, is it constructive or destructive to fear wishing someone a merry Christmas? This doesn't have to be a huge bone of contention—and it shouldn't be. Is the following exchange tense?

> *Merry Christmas, Sam, Brenda,* I say, celebrating the holiday.
> *Happy Hanukah, Vic,* Sam says, not celebrating it.
> *Thanks, have a great holiday,* Brenda says. She's an atheist, but one who isn't threatened by wishing happiness in their celebrations to those who are not and do celebrate.

Everyone is smiling, everyone is staying true to his or her beliefs, and no one is offended. To me, this is a far saner reaction than getting hot under the collar or nasty or rude to one another— or in perceiving a sleight or offense when clearly none is intended.

In all five major world religions, we're taught not to judge. So if all five have this in common, maybe it's because they've hit on something significant. Something universal. And that's a message worth pondering.

Be slow to take offense. It's a sad commentary on what society has allowed itself to sink to when wishing someone "merry" is perceived as offensive. We should think about that.

I have to say that I'm surprised by the level of animosity raised on minor issues such as this. I guess because these reactions are so alien to what comes naturally. How often have you seen a child—the keepers of total honesty—take offense to a happy greeting?

That realization, of course, set me to thinking on the matter because collectively, we say we are proponents of harmony. On this, there has to be an underlying *something* that injects harmony. *But what?*

In exploring, we see that our views are influenced and shaped by personal exchanges on the topics at hand. How we acted. How others reacted. How others acted, and how we reacted to them.

My influence and shaping is largely due to two people: my mother, who loved everyone, regardless of flaws or anything else. She had a great capacity to love and showered it on all people. Others sensed this about her, and that her concern and care for them was genuine. She loved and was loved equally by Hell's Angels and Pastors, Politicians, Welfare recipients, Professors and Ex-Cons. And, yes, I capitalized those because she would have. Everyone was a Capital with my mother.

There's much to be learned from her. Respect for all people, all things. An appreciation for diversity. An innate sense of integrity, and more...

The second influential person is my best friend, who is of a different faith. We've been friends many years, including long before she found her spiritual path in the Wicca religion. So we, the Christian and the Wicca, are best friends. And in all the years of our friendship, there has never, not once, been a challenge between us.

I consider that a significant discovery—hadn't thought of it before—and so I looked back over those past fifteen years, and the reason why there's been an absence of challenges became abundantly clear. We respect each other, and each other's beliefs. We have not always agreed, but we have always agreed to disagree and genuinely meant it.

I'm including this for that purpose—to share that insight. We all walk different paths, but if we respect each other without trying to impose our will on anyone else, then so many of our challenges just disappear. Give it some thought and see if perhaps that insight will assist you in removing some of the relationship challenges in your life.

A good gauge on episodes you encounter is to ask yourself this:

When you're old and you look into the mirror at your reflection, will [insert episode] matter to you?

If it won't matter at that time, then it doesn't matter now. That's a pretty effective gauge at winnowing out all the bull and getting things into perspective. Follow it, and you'll be surprised how many fewer incidents put you in crisis-mode.

Staying out of crisis-mode helps simplify our lives. The gauge also helps us realize the dynamics of what is really happening in these events: a minor identity crisis imposed on us by a select few in society. Someone says we should (or shouldn't) be offended so we are (or aren't.) I say, you have a mind, reason, logic, compassion and you're quite capable of deciding if offense was intended all on your own. You define your perimeters. It's a testing of our own definition of who we are and how we behave. Of what mind-set we consider acceptable or unacceptable.

More often than not, it is a compilation of these non-worthy, anxiety-inducing crises (such as the insignificant door-opening episode) that have us waking up one morning, stumbling to the coffeepot, and wondering who the hell we are. It hits us harder than a double jolt of caffeine that we know we write books, but we no longer know ourselves. Our lives are nothing like we planned, and we haven't got a clue what happened to us, or why we ended up so far off-course.

What's happened is that we've stopped seeing ourselves as ourselves. Everyone around us is reactive, so while it would be more comfortable for us to toss the blame for our identity loss on someone else's shoulders, when we get to bottom line honesty, we've deduced that it belongs squarely on our own. While we might well be someone's spouse, parent, or child, that is not all we are. Not by a long shot.

When it first hits us that we're strangers to ourselves, of course we want to blame someone else. Being a victim is easier, more comfortable for us. We can direct our anger and upset outward, elsewhere, away from us. *Anywhere* away from us. But soon we realize, because common sense forces us to, that we're to blame. We *let* this happen. Others only reacted to our perception of ourselves. The perceptions we projected to them and perpetuated.

It's often been said that others take you only as seriously as you take yourself. Well, it's also true that others expect from you what you have projected to them in the past. (We learn from experience, remember?) Through your actions, words and deeds, you show someone else, everyone else, who you are and what you stand for, and they accept what you're showing them as an accurate representation. Then they react accordingly. Now if they're interacting with you under a misconception, is it possible that it is a misconception you planted in their minds?

What if this wake-up call gets your attention, and you look in the mirror and you really don't like the person you see?

Don't despair. Consider yourself exceedingly lucky. You've got courage; you're capable of change. So do it. John Lilly shares this bit of wisdom to help us make such changes actually happen:

> *In the providence of the mind, what one believes to be true either is true or becomes true.*"

That's the concept. But how do you put it into action?

Again, it's easier than you might think.

It's said often that to cause something to manifest in your life, you must do only three things:

1. Think it.
2. Say it.
3. Act on it.

So create the images of yourself that you choose to create, focusing on positive attributes that depict your respect for you— your body, mind and spirit—your gifts and talents. Create images of yourself that empower you to become a better human being and a better writer than you were before you got this wake-up call. And then do the three things necessary to make them manifest in your life.

This concept, though simple, is effective. The reason it is effective is equally simple.

Thoughts have power.

If you doubt it, go outside and *think* a cloud into moving. With focus, you can move the cloud, merge it with others, or make it dissipate. This never fails to stun young students, yet the reason isn't at all mystical. It's scientific, and it has to do with energy. Everything is made up of energy—every single thing— and that includes thoughts.

When we think negative thoughts—about ourselves, others or events—we attract the negative to us like magnets. For a writer, this can be destructive and also crippling. Creativity can hardly flourish under such circumstances. Many successful writers, to stay successful at writing, avoid anything that interferes with their sense of balance and well being. Many avoid reading reviews and fan magazines or professional trade journals because reading them makes the writers feel like underachievers. They prefer not to be advised of any business aspect concerning them. These writers usually have strong agents, publicists and/or business managers or excellent literary attorneys protecting their interests.

To writers with a business background, this hands-off approach seems strange. But it works for those writers, and they're wise to identify, protect, and nurture their creativity.

Conversely, other writers get intimately involved in every aspect of their writing career. They actively participate in cover art discussions, promotion plans, and marketing campaigns. They strive to understand each step of the publishing process and work to meld their own steps with their publisher's. Knowing what is happening on all fronts is most favorable to these writers. Aware, they are free to be creative. Like the other writers, they are wise to identify, accept and implement ways and means to serve their needs.

Neither way—informed or oblivious—is right or wrong or better. Each way respects the individual writer's preferences and allows the writer to conduct her business affairs in a manner that is harmonious to her nature.

From either perspective, or from any point in between, we see that how we think of ourselves, others, and situations dramatically impacts our lives.

How do we translate this concept into a form fit for daily use? through in all that you do—including in what you write.

A tip: Don't waste your time trying to fake it.

You can't.

Simply put, love yourself or change you until you do. You can't change anyone else, so resist the urge to try. You'll be happier and heaven knows that they will. Besides, you've got a full-time job working on yourself. And translated to your work: Love the work you're doing or change it until you do.

It is so important—vital, critical—to love what you're doing with your life. When you believe in yourself and in what you're doing, it shows in tangible ways and in intangible ways. You can feel your faith's strength in your actions, feel its power and conviction in your heart, and hear its whispers and echoes in your mind. Faith, honor, respect and reverence—all of those positive feelings reinforce your decisions and confirm the goodness in them. This gives you that extra bit of magic and insight that lifts you and your work from the ordinary into the realm of extraordinary. Your enthusiasm, your love, your respect all shine

Many times, over the years, I've seen writers who don't believe in themselves put themselves down. This is not only heart-wrenching to witness, it's devastating because common sense swears you *will* become what you believe yourself to be. Good, bad or indifferent.

What you believe yourself to be...

That poses another question you should ask yourself and answer. Have you defined your mission?

What is a mission?

Definitions are in **Guidepost 7.**

ৰ্হ্নGuidepost 7 ৯৯

Define Your Mission

WE'VE ALL HEARD IT. If you don't know where you're going, how can you get there?

Well, the truth is you can't. It doesn't matter how old or young you are, it's never too late—or too early—to decide who you choose to become or what you intend to accomplish.

But what if you just don't know? How do you figure these things out?

Spend some quiet time alone. Think about them. What are your dreams, your desires? What do you feel passionately about? What do you love? Hate? What makes you happy or sad? What embarrasses or humiliates you? What tickles your fancy—ticks you off? What motivates you, brings out your best? What makes you back off, brings out your worst? Do you know your own hot buttons? The things that leave you cold? What puts fire in your blood and refuses to leave you be until you *do something?*

Remember, knowing what you don't want is just as important as knowing what you want. Use your negative responses to cull and pare, and then focus on the positive responses to help create a content and happy you, who creates works you'll be elated at having associated with you.

By getting to know the whole you—and if it's been a while since you've thought about these things, you do need to get reacquainted with yourself before making decisions about the rest of your life—you give yourself a chance to find out not only who you are, but what you stand for and what you stand against. You get in touch with your dreams. It's making those dreams realities that puts magic into your life. That magic is contentment, and it lifts an adequate storyteller to a gifted one.

Think back to when you were a child. What did you dream about then? As you matured, it's likely that many of your dreams changed, but it's highly possible that some important ones have remained dormant inside of you, just waiting until you were ready to rediscover them, and yourself. Explore now. Assess. Then evaluate and make your decisions about where you choose to go from here, and why you choose to go there.

When I begin teaching a new group creative writing, after introductions, my first question is, "What kind of books do you want to write?"

I'm always amazed that so many writers don't know. Often, I get responses such as, "Whatever kind sells." These writers, unfortunately, haven't yet realized that writing commercial fiction just doesn't work that way. To convey love for a book—its magic—the writer first must feel it. That doesn't come from "whatever sells." It comes from writing about something that inspires the writer. Something that engages—often *enrages*—the tions. That engagement translates onto the page and engages the reader—makes the reader care.

So knowing this, ask yourself:

- What do you want to write?

- What must you accomplish in your career to feel content?

- Must you sell a specific number of copies of your book?
- Must you make a specific bestseller list?

- Be sent on publicity tours?

- Must you produce two novels each year? Four?

- What *exactly* do you want?

That is your mission.

It's important that you let others who play an important role in your life know your mission. If the core group in your life—your family, your agent and editor—all know your goals, then they're not wondering what you want or wishing they could read your mind. They know because you've told them.

This communication can be a wonderful thing. By telling others your goals, you open the door for them to tell you theirs. That generally creates an atmosphere conducive to making collective efforts at attaining combined success. No one is floundering, wondering what s/he should be doing. Everyone is focused—and focused on positive, constructive, *informed* aspirations.

A few years ago, eight writers formed a group. I was fortunate enough to be one of them. Our mission was simple. To get everyone in the group published. For the two of us who already had been published, the goal was to get published again. We worked together, watching out not just for our own interests, but alert to things of interest to the others in the group.

We did it. Books, magazine articles, short stories, newspaper columns, professional, academic point papers—in fiction and nonfiction. Considering some in the group write children's stories, some thrillers, some science-fiction/fantasy, some romance and some literary fiction as well as all the different types of nonfiction, this accomplishment was remarkable. Darned telling, too.

Why did we succeed? Because everyone in the group knew the mission. Everyone focused on the mission. Worked at it. Every individual committed to collective success. We looked out for each other in marketing, crafting, and submitting with the same dedication and care that we experienced in our own work. Devotion and dedication to purpose can produce magnificent results. It's simple and effective.

This concept not only works with writing groups, it works with spouses, bosses and close friends, too.

I once knew a married couple who decided they wanted to divorce. They couldn't afford one. So they defined a mission: a plan to save for a divorce. They discussed it, budgeted, really communicated about strategies for saving for their divorce fund. The time came when they had put away enough money to cover legal fees, but this process had worked so well that they then redefined their mission. They decided to continue to work together to save enough money so that each of them would start their new lives apart with a nest egg.

During this time, when they were working on their missions, this couple made time to talk with each other. They shared their excitement and enthusiasm, their successes and triumphs—and their fears about going on with their lives alone. By the time they had saved the nest egg money and had accomplished their redefined mission, they had to define yet another new one. Why? Because neither of them any longer wanted to divorce.

Odd?

Not really. For the first time in years, they had worked as a team, as a couple. They'd dared to share their dreams *and* their fears with each other. Talking candidly and openly had become something they did not do. So they had lost touch. But in pooling their resources and working together on a specific mission, they found the magic in each other again.

My point in including this is that I hear repeatedly from writers that their spouses or significant others don't understand the creative process, the writer's needs, and they aren't supportive. A potential resolution resides in the story of our divorcing couple. Involve your spouse or significant other. Help educate them in the process so that they do understand and can offer genuine support. Tell them *specifically* what you need.

It goes without saying that you need to be just as dedicated a listener to their needs.

Writers don't have the luxury of working in a linear fashion. Often they're juggling, doing author appearances on Book 1, preparing a promotion plan on Book 2, writing Book 3, and researching Book 4. They're also answering fan mail, ordering supplies so they aren't reduced to answering said mail on paper towels, writing articles for organizational newsletters, preparing speeches and mailings for booksellers, distributors, readers, libraries and school kids. It's common for a writer to be working on all those things at the same time. If spouses don't know this, then how can they be supportive? And why, dear writer, do you hold your spouse accountable for something unknown? Shoes reversed, would you consider being held accountable in that position fair?

This making-people-aware concept also works with children. I need quiet time to write my novels. Long before my children could read, I told them this, and we devised a system that would let them know when it was okay to interrupt me and when it wasn't. We made two red lights out of construction paper.

If the light was green, it was okay to interrupt.

If it was red, then they were to interrupt only if someone was hurt, bleeding, dead or dying.

We set the rules. Everyone knew them, and everyone honored them.

Simple and effective. I accomplished my writing goal—in a shorter than normal time, which gave me more time with the kids—and they helped me to do it. My books became *our* books. Because in helping me, they were active participants in the creative process. No frustration, no hurt feelings, no harsh words or annoyances. Just sweet success.

Definitely a win/win situation for the children and me. And it happened because we all were crystal clear on the mission.

Whether you're discussing your writing career or your life, a mission is a personal thing. No one else can define it for you, nor should they. Your commitment to your mission, your discipline and devotion to it, will determine your success. So listen to the advice and opinions of others, take the good that can be gleaned from them, but in the end, decide for yourself what mission you want to invest in at this time.

And keep that mission as dynamic as you are by periodically reviewing it. We change with each challenge met. With change, we must review and re-evaluate. Has what you wanted remained the same? If not, revise your mission to reflect what you choose to invest in now.

The most important point common sense shares with us on this matter of missions is to consciously decide what we want, to choose. It's so easy to get caught up in the daily details and to just drift. But one day we wake up and it hits us like a sucker punch to the gut that we've drifted through decades of our lives. Stunned, we shake our heads and ask ourselves where the years went—and why the hell we haven't gotten anywhere.

Panic sets in. Panic and regret, and a compelling sense of urgency to do something that matters to us—*now*.

A School of Hard Knocks for Writers Tip:

On a daily basis, prioritize tasks and desires so that those most important to you first get the lion's share of your effort.

Common sense also tells us that we should like our own company. Meaning, we don't fear being alone.

This isn't a challenge for most writers, but at times, it can become one. Armed with knowledge of it, when it strikes, we stand prepared to deal with it constructively.

I once knew a sweetheart of a woman who would get up at the crack of dawn and, before she had her first cup of coffee, she would start phoning friends. She couldn't bear not having someone else with her at all times. She would cook huge meals, have house parties, do all kinds of things to keep other people around her.

It was some time before I realized that her reason wasn't that she loved people. Her reason was that she didn't like herself. In her past, she had done things that she had never forgiven herself for doing. When alone, she thought of them. The constant company of others allowed her to avoid thinking of them—until she was again alone.

The oddity here is that had someone else done those same things, she would have been first in line to forgive them. But she couldn't, wouldn't, forgive herself.

Sad, isn't it?

Avoidance never works because it doesn't fix anything. The problem just sits there and festers, and the wound stays raw. Until she comes to terms with her past and extends to herself the same compassion, courtesy and grace that she would give to others, her wounds will never heal and she will never know peace.

We've all done things that, in retrospect, we wish we hadn't done. But we must learn to treat ourselves as well as we would treat a good friend or a stranger on the street. We're all teachers and students, and experience teaches. So learn, forgive yourself, and accept that the past is done. We can't change it. We can only change what lies ahead of us.

And we can remember that laughter cures a lot of ills. Hang on to your sense of humor. It's as strong as Atlas, and it will carry you through hard times when little else can.

Being gentle with ourselves, and treating ourselves with the same respect and reverence we treat others, is hard for us. We're taught to be tough, self-sufficient and self-sustaining. But the truth is that we all need nurturing.

And that brings us to **Guidepost 8.**

↬Guidepost 8 ↫

Nurture

NURTURE YOURSELF, YOUR FAMILY, your work, your peers.

In years of conversations, I rarely have felt the need to advise anyone to nurture their things. Blessing or curse, we do seem to have mastered that. But when it comes to nurturing ourselves and those most important to us, collectively, we are sorely lacking. We are so lacking at nurturing ourselves, I wonder if we're trapped in a universal void.

As we learned earlier, we are all made up of energy. Energy can be depleted. If we don't nurture ourselves, we render ourselves unable to nurture anyone or anything else. We have nothing left inside us to give.

This concept is particularly hard for Southern women and Catholics to grasp. I suppose because we're raised to feel guilty about everything. But common sense tells us that everything in life deserves reverence and respect. *Everything.* It's inherent. And that includes all of us—*even* Southern women and Catholics.

Nurturing ourselves is *not* a matter of being selfish or self-indulging. It's a matter of attaining and maintaining balance. It's a means of staying in-tune and attuned. When we feel cared for, our proverbial cup runneth over, and then we're equipped to reach out and care for others.

Our caring translates, as does so much about us, into all areas of our lives, particularly in our books. If we nurture the work, it shows. Our agent senses it. Our editor senses it. Our readers sense it. That spurs an instinctive reaction from them. They feel good; we feel good. And we should because in evoking that reaction, we have proven to ourselves that our purpose for writing this particular novel has been effectively conveyed. Conveying effectively is the writer's goal. Success breeds confidence. The quality of the work increases, and the writer is often far more productive, spending less time second-guessing herself and more time writing. Our deeds reflect a caring and a respect that was absent in them before. Everyone benefits. Everything benefits.

I knew a man once who was very devoted to his family. He was a wonderful provider, very dedicated and hard working. He was also a yeller. Not at his friends, of course, or at anyone who could refuse to tolerate his yelling. He chose little victims: his children. He stayed out of family matters while they were going well. He didn't tell his children they were doing well, of course, nor did he ever say he was proud of them, much less that he loved them—though he definitely did. Fiercely. He didn't encourage his children to talk with him about their problems or invite them to share their joys. He did talk *at* them, and he never missed a chance to be critical or to give them hell. He had an eagle eye when it came to seeing their flaws and finding fault, and an acid tongue in letting them know he hadn't missed a thing.

Yet, he did care about his children. He wanted to protect them. He did love them and, over the years, he did do wonderful, selfless things to help his children.

Now, they are grown and the man has passed on. And what do his children remember about him?

> *Dad was always angry, and he yelled a lot. Nothing I did was ever good enough for him, or ever done right. There was no pleasing him. He's the only parent I've ever heard of who could make you feel guilty as hell for making all As—because they weren't A+s.*

With maturity, these grown kids still have the wounds from the verbal stabs they received as children. They remember the thrust of what they lived. Even though they now realize that their dad had not been a content man, the impact of his actions remains. The good he did for them is recalled—with deliberate thought and after the hurt is remembered and relived. There's a lesson for us in that.

If you died today, what would your children think of when they think of you? What would your spouse think of you? Your extended family and friends? Others who matter to you?

Are your honest answers to those questions acceptable to you—the way you want to be remembered by these people?

Nurture. Be firm but gentle with your creations—the ones who breathe and the ones you, the writer, breathe life into on paper. Respect them.

When you finish a book, it is normal to feel a sense of loss, and maybe a little bereft. Perfectly understandable, really. You've been immersed in this project for months, intimately involved in the characters' lives and what's going on with them, and now you are saying good-bye to these people who have come to mean a great deal to you. You've invested physically and emotionally.

The best medicine for this "separation syndrome" is to take a walk, smile at a stranger, say a kind word to someone who looks as if they could use one. Pet a dog, feed the ducks or squirrels or birds. Do something nice for someone else just to brighten her day. And then get started on your next book.

You get out of relationships what you invest in them. You have to do what you feel is right, of course. You also have to fill your proverbial creative well so that there is nurturing and caring inside it to draw out and share with others through your work.

Common sense proves the same is true of life.

Doing what you feel is right: the topic that takes us to **Guidepost 9.**

☙Guidepost 9 ❧

Do The Right Thing

IT DOESN'T MATTER HOW LONG or how deeply you've craved it, how hard you've worked for it, or how much you want it, the best offer in the world still becomes the greatest challenge if you instincts, intuition or that little voice inside you tells you it's wrong.

It doesn't matter what *it* is, or what the offer regards— could be a person, place or thing, or an offer to buy (license, really) one of your books. Regardless, the concept remains valid.

We're all confronted with potential wrongs. Whether they come in the form of being offered a contract to write a book we feel no passion for writing, to change something in a book that we've written, or an opportunity (or a request) to hide a truth.

All of these things, and many more, we sense are wrong. There's a part of us—the human part that has scraped and struggled and strived to achieve a goal and sees this as a helpful opportunity—that's tempted to ignore the warning signs and do these things anyway, but we have to be strong enough, and confident enough, to have the courage to refuse.

Because in these situations, if we accept, we lose. Big.

If a writer feels no passion for a project, then no passion will be conveyed in the novel. Without passion, the work is lifeless, the reader is dissatisfied. If publication should come, which is unlikely, then the editor isn't enthused, the sales staff isn't enthused, and the booksellers aren't enthused. No word-of-mouth encourages sales. And so the writer suffers a lousy sell-through that affects her future sales dramatically.

Who wins?

No one.

Be passionate about the work, or simply tell the editor making the offer the truth. "I can't be passionate about this project. Please, offer it to someone who can do it justice."

Will the writer be penalized?

No. She's lost a sale, that's true, but she's gained far more. She's exhibited integrity and genuine concern over the success of the project.

The writer's net gain?

Respect.

If you're asked to change something in a book that you've written and you innately know that the change is wrong, then explain your rationale clearly and concisely in concrete terms. While an editor/agent has read the work, you've lived with it for months. Share your experience.

Now, ego or an aversion to criticism doesn't come into play here. Often that fresh-eyed editor or agent sees things in the work that the writer can no longer see because the writer is too close, too entrenched in the project. So the wise writer will view the request for revisions as objectively as possible and then, if the change still feels wrong, explain why. The key is in remembering that the writer and editor or agent both want the same thing: the best book possible.

Writing something that leaves the writer unfulfilled will severely impact her creativity and outlook; hence, her life.

Indifference breeds contempt.

Contempt breeds rage.

And rage destroys.

Don't willingly be its victim.

Know that your instinctive reaction in difficult situations is going to be to take the easy way out. To find the lowest point of conflict and run to it. It's tempting. No one, including writers, thrives on confrontation or conflict. But is there really an easy way out?

Maybe so—insofar as the other person involved is concerned. You can run from others, but you can't run from you.

The world isn't big enough. And you aren't small enough to hide. You've got too much character.

Does taking this easy way out sit well on your shoulders? Or does it conjure shame?

If it raises so much as a sliver, then you know your instincts and common sense agree that the easiest road isn't the right one—and in the long run, if you should decide to take it anyway, they'll prove it to you.

Guilt is never pretty. No one wears it well. And it isn't easy to swallow, either. Worse is living with it. That can be sheer hell. So resolve to avoid it.

Face the difficult challenges with dignity and grace, and with integrity. You'll sleep better at night, and write better during the day.

As for the truth. Well, it never stays hidden. Agendas don't, either. Save yourself tons of recrimination and banging your own head against the wall. Simplify. Just resolve to be open and honest, straightforward and truthful in your work—in the writing, in your personal and professional relationships, and in the way you conduct your business affairs.

Hidden agendas backfire. Manipulations breach trust. And both reduce any selflessness into selfishness. Then everything suffers: your relationships, your writing, and you.

Doing the right thing is easy when it doesn't ruffle feathers. It's when it ruffles them hard or plucks them out that the choices become difficult. But even then, common sense doesn't desert us. It leads us to the right paths. We only have to choose to take them.

Knowing we might be forced to endure conflicts and challenges, we have to choose to believe in ourselves and in our convictions, and do the right thing.

In certain areas of our lives, this concept proves particularly difficult for us to embrace. One such certain area is in the simple act of gratitude: **Guidepost 10.**

❧Guidepost 10 ❧

Gratitude

AT ONE TIME, EVERYONE IN THE BUSINESS of writing was a rookie.

Through experience, we grew. And no small part of that experience came to us from the kindnesses of others. From people who took time to share their experience, their knowledge, and their insights. Editors, agents, contest judges, and/or mentor-writers who took time to comment in their rejection letters, shared their experiences through lectures, critiques, and in workshops. We gained experience from those further up the career ladder who shared with us.

This might come as a surprise to some, and it might shock others, but it is the truth. Others owe us nothing. Editors and agents do *not* owe writers rejection letters *with comments*. Other writers are *not* obligated to share their knowledge. These are gifts. Gifts of precious commodities: their time, their energy, and their expertise.

I'm sorry to have to say it, but too often we repay these kindnesses with complaints. Common sense tells us this is wrong, and it's right to do so. Even if we don't agree with what an editor, agent, judge or mentor-writer tells us, we should acknowledge that them saying anything at all is a gift. An attempt to help. And we should be grateful for it.

I read a column in the newspaper recently that made me think. The columnist was elated because he had received an actual handwritten note. At first, I shrugged it off, not seeing the significance of this. But then I thought about how much the way we communicate has changed. We don't write letters anymore, we email. We seldom write thank you notes, or much of anything else by hand. And then the truth hit me. What the columnist found significant wasn't truly the handwritten note, it was the personal touch, the moment of holding the complete attention and focus of another person that the handwritten note symbolized.

We all respond to the personal touch. To the little blessings.

When was the last time you thanked someone for helping you?

When is the last time that you thought about or acknowledged that someone who helped you wasn't required to assist you—even to yourself?

When was the last time you counted your blessings?

A caveat for many writers is that we either don't focus at all on what we want, or we want so much else that we fail to appreciate all of the wonderful things we already have. Whether the reason is a wildly ambitious streak in us, or a hectic lifestyle, we don't stop and smell the roses.

We don't enjoy our blessings.

Resolve today to smell the roses—every petal—and their leaves and stems. If the writing goes well, be grateful for it. If not—and here's the challenge—be grateful for that, too. It could be that you've got a plot problem heading your way in a couple of chapters and your subconscious has recognized it and is attempting to make you consciously aware of it so you can begin working to resolve it.

One year for my birthday, a dear friend gave me a journal. She said that it wasn't an ordinary book; it was special. *A Blessings Book.* I should note all the good things in my life in this book, and then, when I was feeling down, I should go back and read them. This would help me to see how many blessings I have, and how many blessings I have enjoyed.

She was right.

When we focus on the future, we neglect the present. When we focus on the past—which we cannot change—we neglect the present. Common sense tells us to learn from the past and then put it to bed, and to consider the future, but to live in the present.

It's right, too.

Buy a Blessings Book—a tablet will do. Write down the things that happen in your life that make you feel special, blessed, and grateful. I can tell you this, you'll be surprised at what you write when you go back later and read. It's not the big things. Those, I've found, are the briefest notes. The richest entries are the blessings and my gratitude for the little things. Like the time my eighteen-year-old daughter had been home for a week with chicken pox. She had a serious case of cabin fever, and she was giving everyone around her a serious case of "Please god, cure her before I lose it" fits. In my Blessings Book, I wrote: *Scabs and all, Krissie smiled today.*

I still smile and feel a little heart tug on reading that.

Little things *do* matter. And if you choose, this Blessings book becomes an heirloom of memories. The kind you swear you'll recall forever when they happen but get lost under the weight of daily life.

When it comes to negative feelings, little things still matter. We start out being confronted with a gnat-size annoyance. Then we mull on it, feed it, give it energy.

The more energy we give it, the larger it grows—and looms. What had been a minor, mild annoyance now is irritating, and unless we refocus our attention, we're going to end up in a negative black hole, a pit of despair. It takes a lot of attention to slither around a pit long enough to find a way out and even more energy to crawl out. Such a struggle—and it started with a mild, minor annoyance, a molehill that we made a mountain.

The more energy you give something—positive or negative—the more powerful it becomes. Feed a negative thought and it grows. If we continue to feed negativity in our minds, this gnat-size annoyance explodes into a full-blown crisis. We feel that hell has come to call.

Worse, that we've summoned it.

We must change our perspective.

Focus not on the problem, but on the solution to the problem. Not on what can't be done, on what can be done.

Turn a negative into a positive.

That redirects our energy—focusing on the positive—and we spare ourselves from feeling helpless and frustrated and overwhelmed. We're not victims of our own negative thoughts anymore because we chose to change. We determined when it made sense to keep thinking about something and feeding it our energy, and when it was time to change our thinking, our perspective of the challenge.

It's a far healthier view.

Let's be frank. Writing a book is never easy. And anyone who claims that it is has experienced a miracle and has no conception of the hand-wringing, hair-pulling, gut-wrenching challenges that normal writers deal with constantly. May they forever be graced and never experience the reality!

But for the rest of us, we struggle, limp—at times, crawl—to get just the right words in just the right phrases to create a fictional dream in which the reader is totally immersed from start to finish. If we're lucky, though the writing is challenging, it will appear seamless and effortless to the reader.

Sometimes we are lucky. Sometimes we are not. And when we are not, then we must know when to stop and take stock. We must know when to quit, which brings us to **Guidepost 11.**

✋Guidepost 11 ❧

Know When to Quit

AT TIMES, WE ALL GET ON THE WRONG PATH. Recognizing we're on it, of course, is the challenge or we   wouldn't be there. So how do you recognize it?

Common sense suggests you slow down and look at where you are. Have you stayed true to your mission, or have you lost focus and strayed off-course? Have you devised a concrete plan of action for getting where you choose to go, or are you aimlessly drifting? Can you see your destination clearly inside your mind?

A few years ago, a good friend of mine who writes captivating, award-winning novels had one of those *I hate my life* revelations and decided to change it. She made a book out of a loose-leaf binder.

In it, she put magazine photos of things she chose to have in her *new* life.

- Photos of a hard cover novel (upon which she inserted her name and the title of a book deemed too risky to sell in the present market).
- A house.

- A car.

- A new bread-making machine.

- Pictures of her children, looking happy and content; of her husband at work, healthy and happy, and at home, working in his garden (his passion).

- A new computer, representing her dream of writing full-time.

- An exercise bike, representing a conscious effort to exercise and take better care of herself.

- Photos standing as symbols for patience and serenity.

With each photo, she included an index card, upon which she wrote a brief remark of why that photo had been included and what it meant to her.

Then, she prioritized these photos and images, so that the ones she considered most valuable and important to her appeared first in her book.

Now she has acquired most of these things, and she's developed a specific plan for achieving the others or acquiring them.

This writer made specific, concrete choices. She took control, focusing on the positive. She focused on her mission.

And it's working!

Note that all of the things she included in her book were tangible. There were entries representing body, mind and spirit— the whole person. This is an important lesson to all of us. If we image the mind, body and spirit that comprises each of us as a three-legged stool, with one leg representing each aspect of us, then we can grasp the value in balance and harmony quickly and easily. If we shorten any one of the legs, the stool wobbles and rocks. But if each leg is the same length—treated with equal respect and reverence—then it's balanced. We are balanced. Each leg supports its weight and makes the whole stronger, capable of bearing more weight more efficiently.

Now, what if you have stayed true to your mission, stuck to your concrete plan of action, and you have a firm fix on your destination, and yet you're still hitting brick walls?

Don't panic. All this means is that you've reached a turning point.

Turning points are as natural a phenomenon in your career as a writer as they are in your life. As we grow and change, we fulfill our goals. That brings us to a time of new goals, new challenges—a turning point.

Change happens, and it's often scary, often difficult, but it is always for our own greater good. If we fight it, change still comes, though it's harder on us and can bring with it unnecessary *growing* pains. But if we work with change, then the transition is far more palatable and peaceful for us. We're working with ourselves rather than battling ourselves during the transition.

So you recognize that you're on the wrong path. Now the question becomes:

Where do you turn?

The answer isn't mystical or scientific. It's simple—for common sense. Where you turn depends on where you choose to go from here. If you know the answer to that, then you know where to turn. If you don't know the answer, then you're confronted with choices—and likely, with confusion.

While the same concept applies for relationships and in other areas of your life, let's stick with writing to illustrate. Let's say you have an opportunity to switch careers and do something totally different.

Look within.

If you can quit writing, then do it. If you can put down your pen, walk away from writing and feel no regret, then by all means do it. If you love writing, which truly is the *only reason* worth spending a third of your life doing it, you won't be able to quit. And that is the fastest way to define the desires hiding in the deepest recesses of your heart.

But what if you can't quit, you do love writing, and yet you've lost the enthusiasm you once had for your work?

What if you've been writing a specific type of novel and now suddenly you've started getting rejection letters on everything you submit? What then?

Know that you are not the only one in the world who has faced this problem. Unfortunately, it's common. Your gut reaction is to place blame—on the editor, your agent, the market—even if none deserve it. Very often the writer's answer to what is wrong can't be found anywhere *out there*. The answer lies within.

So look within. Whatever the cause, this is a signal to the writer that it's time for change. *Whoa, wait*, you say. *Change? I can't change. Change to what? I've developed a career. I can't just walk away from it.*

I say you can walk away. And the reason you can is simple. If there is no passion, then no passion can translate from you onto the written page. If no passion translates, then no editor, agent, or reader gets enthused, and that equates to *no sale*. So if there's no sale, what *exactly* are you walking away from?

More rejection letters. More self-doubt. More negativity wreaking havoc on your creativity and sense of worth. Are those bad things to avoid? Of course they are.

Far more important than dwelling on the loss is to discover where your passion went. What do you feel passionate about writing? It could be that you simply need to take stock, to be nudged into stretching your creativity within your current type of novel writing. It could be time to expand your writing to include other types of novels, to take on new challenges.

Or it could be that you're being signaled to expand your thinking about what you're writing and why.

Whether you continue to write the same type of novel, or you move on to another type of writing, you've redefined your mission. You've taken a hard look at what you're doing, and you've reiterated its value to you and to others.

All of these events are constructive, productive, and they all happened because you reached a turning point.

You knew when to quit. And because you did, odds are high that you recognized   potential. That's the topic in **Guidepost 12.**

✥Guidepost 12 ✥

Recognize Potential

WE'RE FULL OF IT, our work is full of it, and others are full of it.

See the potential in yourself, in your work and in others. Give it its due. Encourage and support it. Remember, *Image it, and it will be.*

I've forgotten who first said that, but from the moment I heard it, I've carried its power in my head and heart. It reminds me that possibilities are limitless—if we allow them space in our lives in their natural form. And that it is through our thoughts, actions and deeds that we limit ourselves where there are no limits.

So give yourself permission to explore your possibilities and your potential. Encourage others to explore theirs. Praise their efforts, and your own.

Back when God was a baby and I was in elementary school, I was taught the planets in our solar system in their orbital order from the sun. I still, all these years later, recite them that way: Mercury, Venus, Earth, Mars, Jupiter, Saturn, Uranus, Neptune, and Pluto.

If your goal is Pluto, then don't shoot for Jupiter. You concentrate, focus on and aim for Pluto.

Now you might not make it Pluto. You might only get to Uranus. But you'll have gotten two planets farther than if you'd aimed for Jupiter.

The key point I'm trying to make is that if you shoot for brass, you're never going to strike gold. Start wherever you are now. Set your sights higher, farther. Recognize that your potential is a gift to you that's meant to be used wisely. Accepting that you have it isn't bragging or being full of yourself. We all need to know our strengths. And denying that you have potential certainly isn't wise.

Whether gold to you is to write the best damn category novel ever or to make the *New York Times* list with a blockbuster thriller, shoot for it.

And remember, brass tarnishes.

Start wherever you are. That's **Guidepost 13.**

⋖Guidepost 13 ⋗

Start Wherever You Are

WHEN WE BEGIN OUR LIVES, none of us are qualified to do anything, much less to write a book.

Accept it.

Then write the book.

Expecting that we must be qualified before making an attempt is as unreasonable as expecting to live an entire lifetime without making even one mistake. We *all* make mistakes and, unlike puberty and acne, we don't outgrow our penchant for making them. As kids and teens, we tell ourselves that when we grow up and have children, we aren't going to make the mistakes our parents made with us—and so we don't. We make different ones.

As new writers, we say we aren't going to make the same mistakes we've noted in other authors' works. And we don't. Like parents, we make different mistakes.

We're never perfect. Life itself is not perfect. It's messy, and so are we. For as long as we live, we are going to commit wrongs, if only minor ones. And that's okay. We didn't get a guidebook at birth, and any instruction manuals we've gotten since then were written by humans, mentors and guides who, for all their good, are flawed by human imperfections, too.

Resolve yourself to learning as you go, understanding that learning is a lifelong, continuous process. Answers *will* come as you seek them. There's an old saying that the teacher will appear when the student is ready. It got to be an old saying because it's true. Believe it. Take joy in learning, in each step you take, in every new technique or method that you attempt. Congratulate yourself when you avoid making the same mistake a second time—that's progress! And listen to common sense's warning that if you wait until you feel qualified to start writing a book, you'll die of old age in the starting blocks on Chapter One.

This day, this moment, that's what we've got. That's for certain.

A few years ago, my mother took ill. She lay in the hospital for nearly seven months, and I spent a lot of time with her. Toward the end, she realized death was coming and, though she'd been a wonderful mother, a good wife, and a good friend who always put the needs of others before her own, as her condition worsened, on several different occasions, she fleetingly expressed regret.

That regret wasn't about her work.

It wasn't about her things.

Not once did she mention any of the *stuff* she had spent a lifetime collecting.

Her regret was that she could have been a better person and done more to serve others.

Hearing this from her stunned me. She truly was a remarkable, gracious and giving woman, who reached out to help others even if it meant doing without herself. But her admission sobered me and forced me to accept the truth. If this regret could happen to her, then no one is exempt. No one.

Common sense constantly tells us to take joy in the journey. But we need to expand our thinking to include beyond the journey. Because when the journey is over and we reach our destination, then we've reached the end of life as we know it.

We're more fortunate than many. We've learned this lesson now, not on our deathbeds. Now, while there is still time to change. We're offered this opportunity to choose whether or not we want to look back on our lives and regret.

Priceless lesson, that. As is learning that holding on too tightly chokes: the topic of **Guidepost 14.**

↜Guidepost 14 ↝

Holding On Too Tightly Chokes

SOME WRITERS WILL CONSIDER THIS CONCEPT unpopular. Others will vehemently disagree with it. But I feel passionately about it, so I'm including it.

Some writers hoard what they have learned about writing out of fear that they'll be training their competition and that competition then will take their place in the market, just as some people hoard their possessions out of fear that they will give away too much and end up lacking themselves. To me, this hoarding has two effects, and both are negative.

1. The hoarder deprives the student yearning for knowledge.
2. The hoarder denies herself the potential for being infused with fresh bursts of enthusiasm and perspectives that can offer new insights.

The hoarder has worked hard to gain skills, insight, an edge. She doesn't want to be replaced by someone she's trained. She doesn't want to stand in the dust and watch someone she's trained pass her up on the career ladder. Yet in hoarding, every-one loses. There is no selflessness; therefore the soul is robbed, left hungry. And if you think the impact of that isn't significant, well, it is significant. Ask anyone still searching for contentment and their purpose.

The key is for the experienced writer to understand this simple truth:

A writer can share her loaf of bread, but only the slices that the student is prepared to eat and chooses to eat, can be eaten. You can't share a whole loaf.

The reason you can't share a whole loaf is simple.
We're all equal.
We're all home to specific gifts and strengths.
We're also all on different paths, unique, and no two of us ever see anything in exactly the same manner or light.

So whether you're an experienced writer or a brand new student, share all you can selflessly. The best comes from the collective.

Train your competition. Give them your very best. Because in doing so, you've helped to elevate their standards *and* your own. And when you elevate standards, what happens?

The whole becomes better, wiser, stronger and more effective. Who benefits, then?

Everyone.

Common sense warns that none of us are experts at everything. There are times when we are teachers and times when we are students. All of us. As a parent and creative writing teacher, I freely admit that I've learned an awful lot from my kids and from my students. Have you learned from yours?

When you teach, give of yourself and your knowledge gladly. Maybe, when you're doing your student stints, a teacher will graciously share her knowledge with you. Odds are good— particularly if that teacher is familiar with The Big Picture concept in **Guidepost 15.**

ೞGuidepost 15 ೞ

The Big Picture

WHEN A FRIEND OR SOMEONE in your writing group is offered a new contract and you can't find a publishing home, it's easy to feel envious.

When your publisher makes you a fair offer for a novel, it's easy to feel greedy and want more.

But both are as wrong as envy is negative and destructive.

We all have a purpose, and none of us know each other's. We might know another's goals, but not their purpose. Something that we perceive as good well might be bad, just as something we perceive as bad well might be good. We really don't know what tragedy might have been avoided. We don't know what opportunity will come in the wake of something "bad" that couldn't have come without it. We really can't judge something as good or bad because we have too limited a perspective.

And it is for that reason that we should consider all events opportunities—even those that are unwelcome.

It is also why we shouldn't envy others. Because we don't see their big picture. Hell, more often than not, we don't see our own.

Common sense tells us to be happy for others when they're happy. Even if their perspectives are limited, they do have the best view of their big picture. And if you make a "steal of a deal," don't pat yourself on the back. You might contract that steal but living with the contract will convince you that the real bargain to celebrate is had in striving for a "fair" deal.

In a fair deal, everyone is satisfied and content with the terms. Everyone feels an affinity to bring the project to fruition, to commit to its success. There's balance and harmony, good will and unity of purpose. There's value and appreciation and respect for the work, the other person, and for you.

There's understanding of the big picture.

All interested parties accept that the sum is greater than the individual parts—and that responsibility isn't a coat: the subject of **Guidepost 16.**

⋞Guidepost 16 ⋟

Responsibility Isn't a Coat

RESPONSIBILITY IS LIKE SKIN. You can't pull it out of the closet when it's convenient, you've got to wear it all of the time. And you've got to feel comfortable wearing it.

If you goof up, don't shove it off as someone else's fault. Admit it. Apologize and take the hit for it. Do what you can to fix any problems created by your error—*forgive yourself*—and then go on, wiser for the experience.

Writers affect lives. Those of our families, our friends, other writers, people we socialize with, people we do business with, people we encounter on the streets, and people who read our books.

We affect *those* people *and* the people they affect.

A good number of years ago, I was diagnosed with Graves' disease, which is to say, I have a wacky thyroid gland. One of the side effects was that I got what's called thyroid stare. Normally, your eyelid covers the white of your eye from the lid down to the iris. But when you've got thyroid stare, it doesn't. You look a little bug-eyed. In my case, it was a lot bug-eyed be-cause it took a long time to diagnose the disease and by the time doctors did, the damage was done and it was permanent. Any-way, I was in San Francisco, walking along the pier, and a mime stepped into my path, took one look at me, frowned and stretched his eyes wide.

I'm sure he's long since forgotten the incident. I'm certain he forgot it minutes after it happened.

I still remember it.

I know the mime wasn't being malicious. He saw and reacted. He didn't stop to think that I might be sensitive or uncomfortable about it. Truthfully, I couldn't stand looking in the mirror in those days, because when I did, I saw a stranger's face. The change was fresh, the wound raw, and intentional or not, his bug-eyed stare rubbed salt into it.

It's been twenty years since that event happened. It doesn't hurt anymore, and hasn't for a long time. I've had surgery that has nearly rectified the problem. But I haven't forgotten that incident, or how it made me feel.

I vowed that day to become more attuned to the feelings of others. So this painful experience proved to be a valuable lesson for me. In a very real sense, that mime changed my life.

And that is the common sense point here.

Often, we don't realize the impact of our actions on others, and we should be aware. Whether or not we are aware, or our actions are accidental or intentional, we must accept the truth. Pens are very powerful and influential tools. We wield them, and in doing so, we change lives.

Many writers know this from fan letters, where readers cite how our novel opened their eyes, made them take a second look at their spouse and decide he wasn't so bad, after all. Letters where the reader pours out her pain, her deepest secrets and greatest fears and tell the writer how her novel offered an opportunity for the reader's own beliefs and values to re-emerge in her life. Letters that say our novels offer constructive solutions to problems and proof to readers in similar situations that there is light at the end of their dark tunnels.

Changing someone's life is a powerful thing. It's a blessing and a responsibility that no writer should take lightly or without thought. The gift of having the ability to initiate or be a catalyst for this change bears with it the obligation to acknowledge the potential impact. And that demands that the author write with passion *and* compassion.

That the author understands that responsibility isn't a coat.

And that truth proves to us that success *is* in how you play the game: **Guidepost 17.**

❧Guidepost 17 ❧

Success *Is* in How You Play the Game

LIFE ISN'T A GAME. But if we equated it to one, then whatever success we glean from life would be in how we played the game of it.

If we walk over other to get where we want to go, participate in shady deals, let greed alone rule our negotiations, hoard our knowledge, and express no gratitude for the efforts and sacrifices others make on our behalf, then we leave others trampled and we short ourselves. Is that success? Is that the way we choose to live our lives? Knowing that we trampled others and shorted ourselves?

It's a no-brainer that common sense says no. It's only when we act in good faith and fairly—in crafting our work, in our relationships, in our collective efforts to market and sell those works—that we attain success and have truly accomplished. Because it is only then that we've allowed our thoughts, actions and deeds to permeate our lives and our works fulfill us. We're outwardly reflecting what we believe inwardly.

Harmony.

No success should ever feel hollow. But fulfillment requires its dues.

That we pay them defines our character—us.

And we define our lives.

So our success *is* a direct result of how we play the game.

Now, sometimes we do our best to play this game fairly and others attempt to refuse to let us. We feel that they deliberately and willfully seduce us into not being fair and not acting in good faith. What do we do then?

There is a way to deal with these situations and still retain the ability to look into the mirror and like what you see. By loving 'em through it—the topic in **Guidepost 18.**

৶Guidepost 18 ৸
Love 'Em Through It

ALL WRITERS FACE CHALLENGES.

- Too much to do, too little time.

- Orphaned by your publisher.

- Can't get your dream agent to look at your work.

- Can't submit to your targeted editor without an agent.

- Too many interruptions by phone solicitors and well-intentioned family members during your creative cycle.

- Too many intrusions from other areas, cutting into your writing time.

- Terminal hold on submissions.

- Too many occurrences in the business end of your writing career where you have *no* control.

And that's just naming a few!

We get frustrated, disappointed, exasperated, irked, aggravated, and on occasion, downright outraged.

We're human, so that's okay. Yet we know that sustaining these negative feelings is counterproductive and that they can lead to destructive problems for us—and for those making us feel those emotions. But becoming a screaming shrew isn't going to make any writer feel better. It's been tried. It failed. It makes the writer feel worse. And being confronted by a screaming shrew certainly isn't going to inspire our victims to feel better. So what will?

The key to solving that riddle is in realizing that writers don't need a chip on their shoulder. They need an attitude adjustment.

When everything is going right, it's easy to love others. It's when your world is turned topsy-turvy, you're frustrated and certain no one on the planet understands you; when the kids are acting like aliens—spoiled brat aliens—your spouse is as sensitive to your needs and frustrations as a dead stump, and you're sick and tired of demands—and of being sick and tired— that it's hard to love anyone—especially yourself. But it is exactly then that everyone needs love most—including you.

There is no honor or glory or dignity in loving only the loveable, or in loving only when the mood strikes you. Especially when others disappoint you.

It's when we take that tough next-step, expecting nothing, doing good just for goodness' sake and love them *anyway* that we gain the most good.

Whether or not the world notices our good deeds doesn't matter. Whether or not our loved ones notice them doesn't matter. *We* notice. *We* know. And even if no one else cares, *we* care.

We're enough.

In novels and in life, loving and caring are two of the riskiest ventures a human being can undertake. There are no guarantees you or your work will be loved back or even appreciated. There are no promises that you won't be hurt. Actually, common sense leans toward figuring that if you love someone long enough, they're bound to hurt you to some extent because human beings, by fluke or design, tend to do that to one another with monotonous regularity.

So when it happens, take solace. We love. We're enough. We decide what to take into ourselves and how deeply we take anything inside us. We can't control others' actions, but we can control our reactions to their actions. We can make choices that are healthy for us.

All self-employed people, and some who are not, face time challenges. Successful people become skilled at time management—even if the idea of having to appalls them. They learn to prioritize tasks daily so that what is most important gets done first, and they learn to minimize non-essential commitments.

Not every hour of the writer's day should be scheduled. Creative people require time to daydream and to mull over *life, death and the universe* issues.

Writers need down time, too. And not just when they're ill, which is how the body signals that it needs a break when it doesn't get a break without illness. Feeding the creative muse is as vital to writers as the air that they breathe. Respect it. Manage, and simplify.

Being orphaned, failing to get that dream agent to read the work, and being restricted from submitting to a targeted editor without an agent can be frustrating. Actually, it can be worse. But it does help the writer to know that all writers go through difficult times. All writers suffer setbacks—some of their own making, some not—and some who had elevated themselves in their careers are forced to start over, writing a different type of novel or writing under a pseudonym.

Starting over doesn't seem constructive, and yet it often is constructive *and* lucrative. Let me share an example.

A romance writer lost her editor. The new editor and this author were creatively incompatible. This writer had come to a turning point and accepted it. She not only changed publishing houses, she took a leap of faith and wrote a book she'd wanted to write for a long time—a mystery. It not only sold but it was extremely well received in the market. Now, four books later, this author is a national bestseller.

Though the transition itself must have been a difficult one that likely produced its fair share of anxiety, I'm sure as certain this author doesn't regret once being orphaned—not now!

It's said by many that getting an agent is more difficult than getting an editor.   The important thing for a writer to remember here is to aim for the right agent. A dream agent for another writer could be a nightmare for you. It doesn't matter how successful the agent is, how many connections he or she has, how good he or she is agenting for others, if that agent isn't enthused about your work and extremely determined to help you meet your goals, then he or she is not *your* dream agent.

Choose your associates carefully and wisely based on concrete criteria that are specific to you. You're not marrying the agent, so it isn't a *take the bad with the good* relationship. Find a strong agent with the assets and abilities to do what you need done.

Often writers who want to secure a specific agent or editor will attend writing conferences where that agent/editor will be and attempt to get appointments with them, either through the conference or outside it. Other ways to break down submission barriers are to request referrals from writers you know who are familiar with your work and currently work with that editor/agent. Enter contests where the editor/agent is judging. Network. If this door is meant to open for you, you'll find the key to it. You need only seek it.

Many   authors   complain   about   constant   phone interruptions.   There is a simple solution to this challenge. During the time you're in create-mode, turn off the ringer. If that isn't feasible, then invest in an answering machine—and use it.

We discussed family interruptions earlier—kids and the red light—but we need to look at this situation from their perspective, too.

Writers tend to immerse. To get deeply involved and to be singularly focused. During deadlines, it's not uncommon for our families to see no more of us than the backs of our heads, as we sit at the computer or desk and work away. Perhaps we're present at meal times, though often we are physically present and mentally in *la-la land* (as my husband calls it), still immersed in our book.

We need to understand that our non-writing family members don't grasp the creative process. They don't get it that if they interrupt us—even if it's just for a second—then we can't just dive right back into the book and pickup where we left off when interrupted. They have no idea that we must backtrack, try to get back to where we were mentally. Often we lose the thread, our train of thought, or that perfect phrase permanently, which irritates us.

To minimize irritation to us and to help our family stay in our good graces, we need to explain the creative process to them so that they do understand that things like interruptions do carry consequences and ramifications.

And we need to be frank about what we need from them. We also need to be cognizant of what they need from us, and we need to work together to find a fair and reasonable balance.

Now what if you're involved in a professional association and it just isn't working?

Some try to ignore it, which cures nothing and serves as a breeding ground for the development of more challenges and more resentment. So what do you do?

Face the challenge.

Tread easy, weigh all facets of the situation, and then do what you must do to bring about resolutions that restore peace and harmony in your life. If you must sever the association with an agent you've worked with for years, leave the editor that you've worked with through five books, withdraw from a writer's group where you're a charter member, then do it. But before you do, remember that it is easy to find fault with others and to deny any fault is your own. Have your expectations been realistic? Reasonable? Objective and fair?

With a gutful of frustration, it's easy to be blinded to truth and to walk out rather than work at resolving differences. Severing these professional associations are akin to divorce in that respect, and statistics prove in those cases, people would rather switch than seek solutions.

Do yourself a kindness. Break the statistical barriers and seek equitable solutions. It takes effort and will to stay and work at a relationship. Yet any professional association worth forming is worth the effort of making it work.

Whether or not you agree with that rationale, you do need to work at repairing the relationship in the association rather than just cutting and running at the first sign of trouble. If you don't, you'll regret it later, and regret is merciless. It'll chew you up inside. It's far healthier for all involved parties to deal constructively with the matter now.

Do your best to repair the breaches in the association—honestly working at it—and then if you can't, you'll leave knowing that you did everything you could do. There's solace in that. Dignity, too.

Communicate honestly, openly, from a standpoint of *we* and not *I* or *you.* Pointed fingers and laundry lists that blame the other person for difficulties isn't going to fall on receptive ears. Nor is that going to produce an environment conducive to healing breaches.

State your goal: fixing the problems in the association so that you both are content with the outcome. Talk through your differences, focusing on solutions and resolutions. Be respectful and fair. Give your associate an opportunity to absorb what you're saying and your suggestions—and an open forum for responding and interjecting their views and opinions. Encourage them to speak their thoughts. It's this open exchange that offers the potential for resolutions, solutions, understanding and healing.

The thing we tend to forget is that few of us are mind readers. What we think others want or need isn't often what they think or what they want or need. Doesn't it drive you up the wall to be told what you think? What you want? What you need? What is best for you? As if someone—anyone—outside you knows you better than you know yourself. Impossible!

And yet it is extremely common for us to expect others to *just know.* Why? I have no idea, but I do know that it's an unreasonable expectation on our parts. It's damned unfair, too. When we do this, we're expecting more from others than we expect from ourselves.

Work hard, with devotion and commitment, to healing the little breaches as they occur. Tell your editor that you're disappointed with the copyedits, the cover, the promotion done on your book. Accept her telling you that she's disappointed in the revisions you've done, or in the manuscript that you've produced and she'd bought on proposal. Little problems are much easier to resolve than big ones. Why wait until the pressure builds to an explosive level? Then, you're condemned to dealing with mammoth fallout!

In the same spirit of open communication, tell the editor that you appreciate the copyeditor catching an embarrassing mistake, that the cover is terrific, and you're delighted with the promotion plans for your novel.

Talk *and* listen. And never let the other party believe that what they think and feel doesn't matter or that it isn't important. Tell them what you expect, what you hope for, and encourage them to do the same. Love 'em through it—especially when it's hard.

Anyone who writes knows that, at times, it *will* be hard. At times, it *will* be damned difficult. But do it, because the benefits of investing in your professional relationships are worth the effort. They will enrich your life.

If you've tried repeatedly to resolve your differences—done everything humanly possible in your own mind—and the association still isn't working, then you must choose:

1. **Live with the situation as it is, without resentment or bitterness.**
2. **Summon the courage to walk away and start over elsewhere.**

Starting over does require courage. Know it. Accept it. Making your way in an unknown world is daunting. But it's also exciting.

Which bears the most weight in your case?

Daunting?
Exciting?

That depends on you and your attitude. If you know in your mind and in your heart that you've done all you can to salvage the relationship, then be at peace with that. And with yourself. Feel good about your conduct. You took the hard road; you tried—really tried. It didn't work, and that's sad, but the inescapable truth is that you made the effort.

It's customary in this situation, unfortunately, for us to feel that we've failed. But have we? Staying, working at it, not just walking out at the first sign of trouble—all those things strengthen us and define our character. That's not failure. That's personal growth. And growth is success.

We learn from challenges and difficult relationships, but when the lesson is learned, it is learned. Once we grasp the lesson and recognize its value, once we realize the relationship has turned toxic for all parties and that makes it destructive, then common sense tells us it's time to change. We've done our best to repair the breach and fix the broken parts. If we did, wonderful. Everyone is better off for the effort and benefits. If we couldn't, then done is done and it's to summon the courage to treat ourselves and our associates with the respect and dignity every human being deserves and end the association.

That, too, is loving 'em through it.

Many professional associations fail. Some parties disassociate due to changes in the market, changes in focus—the publisher's or the writer's—changes in the industry. The associates have no quarrel to settle or differences to resolve. But there are other associations that fail due to creative differences, and those we should discuss.

Unfortunately, once the association is dissolved, some feel it's necessary to drag their former associate's reputation, judgment and actions through the proverbial gutter. This is an innate reaction and a self-defense mechanism that some use to justify their actions and to prove to themselves and to others that they were wise to sever the relationship. Sadly, many don't think this through to see the end result of their actions.

Dragging a former associate through the gutter *can* undermine third-party respect and trust in an associate, but it definitely undermines third-party respect and trust in the individual doing the dragging. Undermining respect and trust does *not* constitute a good foundation in any relationship.

The dragger well might have valid ethical complaints. If so, she should seek recourse through appropriate channels, handling the situation with dignity and in a professional, non-destructive manner.

When creative differences occur, it's easy for severed associates to feel they must compete for approval. In a word, don't. Before the severance, did you worry about this? Likely not. There was no personal competition then—you were a team. Think about this. Until now, you appreciated hearing positive comments about your former associate. There's no reason—aside from you creating trouble due to your own insecurities—to believe that things must be different now.

Look around. You won't have to look far to see how many walking wounded writers, editors and agents are out there because they suffered from the negative impact of indiscretions encountered as a result of severed professional associations. Learn from the physicians. *First, do no harm.*

I'm not advocating that illegal acts or unacceptable ethical standards should be hidden or condoned. I'm saying that if you must sever a professional association, then do it the right way: with respect, dignity and grace.

It won't always be easy.

It will always be right.

Deliberately driving wedges between people is entering a minefield loaded with explosives that, at some time, will detonate. Don't get caught in the blast. And don't ignite the fuse. Everyone involved must live with the affects for a long time.

For various reasons, at times we all feel unlovable. And during those times, we're armed with excuses:

> *I trudged through hell, experiencing this or that.*
> *My associate put me through hell by doing this or that.*
> *My ex-associate destroyed my confidence by doing this or that.*
> *I'm still suffering aftershocks from _____.* *(Fill in the blank here with the problem of your choice.)*

The simple truth is that no one escapes puberty without experiencing something that could fill in that blank. To some extent, we're all walking wounded. While difficult experiences definitely impact our lives, we must decide not to allow them to destroy our lives. We must make a choice. We must take a leap of faith—on ourselves.

We are wiser for our experiences. Though some of them were damned painful to endure, we're now blessed with the insights and benefits of the lessons learned. This alters our perspective, broadens the lens through which we see things.

Whatever wounds you're lugging around *can* heal. Set the rules; define the perimeters on what is acceptable to you and what is not—as a writer, and as a human being. No matter what life slings at you, you can handle it.

If you want to simply your life, decide who you are and what you want, and then work to become it.

Think.

Decide.

Choose.

Trust your judgment, and your decisions.

I am often asked how in the world I accomplish so much on a typical workday. Well, the truth is that I have a secret weapon. One I'll share now with you.

Every morning, I go out on the deck outside my office with my cup of coffee. I hear the birds sing, I watch the squirrels run. I spend quiet time with me, and I say thank you for all the blessings and good things in my life. I mean it sincerely.

This ritual sets the tone for my entire day and, mentally focused on the positive aspects of life, I can then go into my office and write, free from encumbrances.

When you're free, focus comes naturally. You're happy to be doing what you're doing, and when you're happy, you zip through the work without distractions and without negativity clogging up your mind, fighting for attention.

That's the secret. And it sounds simple because it is simple. But it works. Embrace an attitude of gratitude—even for the tough stuff—and give it a shot. You'll see how powerful it is for yourself.

Find your special time and place. Enjoy it. Make your choices and claim your deepest desires as realities in your life. Give thanks for them. You can change. You have the tools. You are a writer with courage.

And common sense.

❦ Bonus Section ❧

⊰Bonus 1⊱
FRAGILITY OF LIFE ... AND DEATH

On the morning of the 18th, I was already sad. It was the 8th anniversary of my mother's death. Those of you who've been with me for a while, know that we were very close. She lived with me, and our roles had reversed. There are no words to describe losing a mother or a child.

So I awakened sad, full of bittersweet memories and tender ones. Memories that tugged tears and wistful smiles. Then I received an email from a fellow writer that her husband had died that morning. He's been sick for a year, and during that time, she's been a rock. A grieving rock, but a rock. I think under those circumstances that's as good as it gets.

So a sad day became doubly so, and I grieved with and for her. The loss of a spouse is horrific. I've seen it too often to deny it or to try to put a positive spin on it. There isn't one. When a loved one is in pain, the cessation of pain is a good thing, but the loss of physical presence to the one left behind is not good. It is one of those things that must be endured and accepted.

I waited a day to phone, she lives a long way away. And I was so relieved to hear her say that she'd taken her first deep breath in a year. For the first time in all that time, she felt peace.

Now that might seem strange to those who haven't experienced the loss of someone beloved after a lengthy illness. But it sounds so very familiar to one who has had that experience. You're so fearful that something will happen or be done that brings more pain that you can't breathe deep or relax. You feel you must always watch, question and protect. A year is a long time to be ever vigilant. A week is a long time to be on high-alert. You don't sleep, you don't eat, you feel uneasy at being off-watch long enough to take a shower. It's not an easy place, or an easy time.

During our conversation, she said she had a wonderful support system helping her through this: her critique group. And I was reminded yet again how fortunate we writers are because we can rely on each other to be there during tough times.

I think back over the past decade, at all the tough times in my life, and the writers who have been there with me, trudging through them. I think back at all the tough times in my writer friends' lives and the writers who have been there for them with me, trudging through them.

I told my darling husband, Lloyd H., about her loss. He knew her darling husband had been sick, of course. I'd been sharing updates on his condition and hers and I got them. But he looked at me with sadness in his eyes and said, how do you stand it? You know so many people who have so many losses.

That set me back on my heels. I thought about it, and I suppose from the outside that is how it looks to others. But the truth is, writers in my arena are a close-knit, large group. We don't do lip service, we care. And when you care, yes, I suppose you do hurt more often, but you also laugh more often. Rather than just experiencing life through your own eyes, you experience a lot of life through their eyes. That's a privilege. One that brings sadness at times, but also joy.

Writers, and those professionally close to them, are a different breed. Maybe opening those veins in writing makes us more emotionally accessible or just willing to care deeply when it'd be safer to not. I don't know. It doesn't much matter in the big picture of things. What does matter is that a friend is hurting and her writer friends are there for her.

It all does make one think. About the fragility of life, yes. But also about the abundance of little recognized blessings in being a writer.

❧Bonus 2❧
BELIEVE, BELIEVE, BELIEVE...

"Believing in yourself is an endless destination. Believing you have failed is the end of the journey." —Author Unknown

It's been a hard day today. We all have them. It isn't that anything is wrong in my life; actually, I'm feeling very blessed. It is a time when many writers are unsettled, uneasy and questioning their path. And knowing it makes it a hard day for me.

There are many hard facts in this business. But there are even more uncertainties. You can depend on little except the unexpected. This makes it vitally important that you find your balance within.

I realize that sounds a bit too Zen for some, but it is a truth. There are certainties I can share, yes. Some are indisputable. Some are relevant only to those who encounter that circumstance. If you write very long, odds are you will encounter that circumstance, regardless of what it is.

Understand a few basics that really aren't taught anywhere, but can help you if you know them going in:

1. Stuff happens. You can line up your ducks and have them all in a pretty row, but before you can dispatch them to work their magic, something will happen to screw up the formation. You can't stop it, can't even slow it down. What you can do is accept it, and press on.

2. Stuff changes. Often stuff totally out of your control. Stuff that you don't want to happen because you're comfortable with the status quo. Stuff you resent. Stuff you don't grasp. Stuff you fear. You can't change it. What you can do is accept it, and press on.

3. Stuff shifts. What worked well last time or last book, doesn't work this time. Reader tastes have shifted. Line focus has shifted. Publisher's reader base has changed. World events have shaped a new model, made what you've done out of fashion, repugnant, revolting. You can't shove shifted stuff back into its old place. What you can do is accept it, and press on.

I guess the point I'm trying to make is that everything changes and most of it is out of our control as writers. We can rail against it, but to what end? We get sore throats and little more. This is why I feel so strongly that we be open to change, open-minded and in our hearts. Change negates stagnation. That's critical to growth and growth is vital to us.

As writers, we share with readers the human experience. If we stagnate, we have shared all we have. If we change, we gain more insights and understanding and experiences to share.

I'm not saying that change is easy. Often it's more than difficult, requires more work, new learning curves—it can be a real pain in the ass. But it is healthy for us as writers and as human beings.

Too often outsiders fall prey to believing that writing is about the money. It's not. If money were our goal, we'd be in other jobs. There are much, much easier ways to earn a living. Money isn't enough to inspire the type of discipline that writing requires. It never has been, and it never will be.

It is purpose that drives the writer. Inspires her. Motivates her to make the sacrifices required, to tolerate the shifts and changes and stuff that happens. To stick with it, keep after it, chasing what even those closest to us call "the dream."

If you're writing, it's a reality. The truth is just that simple, and that complex.

So how do you stay sane during all these applecart upsets? It's easy. You must remember but this:

There is one and only one thing upon which you can depend: the work.

The passion you feel for it, the purpose you fulfill in investing in it—the sum of all your experiences you bring to it.

That you can control. That you can believe in and that believe in yourself, in the unique aspects of you that you bring to the work for your own unique reasons can make all the rest insignificant... if you will it.

You choose. And the choices you make define whether or not you and your writing are on the right path.

ৰ্জBonus 3৯
SURVIVING THE TOUGH TIMES
ON YOUR FEET,
NOT YOUR NOSE

As I start my day, three things are on my mind.

1. First, it is Veteran's Day, and I am grateful to all those who have served and sacrificed so that I might know freedom. I am grateful and humbled by the costs and the willingness of so many to pay them. Might sound trite, but I promise you, it is most sincerely heartfelt.

2. Today I begin again. The diary of a novel is on hold while a new proposal is begun. A *War Games* book, number 5 (I can't believe we're there already!), *Kill Zone*. I know the heroine well, this Dr. Morgan Cabot. She's appeared in *Double Dare* and in *Bulletproof Princess*, if only briefly, and she intrigues me in ways only those who are extremely sensitive to the unspoken and unseen can. I'm eager to begin working with her, seeing inside the complex layers of this woman and how she relates to the world around her. Lord, we all have layers and conflicts within, but she has an extra layer that nudges at me deep inside. I'm not yet sure why, but during the course of the writing, it'll come. It always does.

3. These are challenging days for writers. Book sales are essentially flat, royalties are scarce, and there's an uneasy hush, felt but unspoken, about writing for a living. A small group are

blossoming and growing and enjoying great success, but many are struggling to stay financially afloat. It has always been vital to write for the love of it but in tough times as these—which have come and gone before and will again—we who write are reminded with a wallop the necessity of Absolute Integrity of Intention and Purpose. And this, I find, is that which most claims the attention of my personal, internal compass this morning.

Regardless of what you do professionally or personally, tough times make for tougher times unless you have other, more significant reasons for doing what you do. It's a time for total honesty and openness with yourself and others. A time to know solidly why you're doing what you're doing—the purpose. Your purpose.

If you work just for the money, you're in trouble. If you work to serve a greater purpose and the money is a by-product—even if it's essential to you and yours to sustain home and life—purpose carries you through the tough times with a sense of worth and rightness. Fulfillment and success are not alien to you during these times because they are defined on your terms, by your requirements.

It is amazing how peaceful purpose and absolute integrity, open honesty, can render you even in the face of turmoil. It isn't that you're unconcerned about the state of things. It's that the state of things isn't all you're concerned about. You're still, through it all, fulfilling purpose. There is an innate beauty in knowing it that has strong soothing powers that allow you to continue working in spite of challenges, regardless of negativity and images of doom and gloom being cast from all directions. They're there and you see them, but they lack the power to knock you to your proverbial knees because you see them AND so much more. The good in what you're doing. The grace in accepting what is and remaining focused on what it is you've chosen to do with your life.

During tough times, some quit. Relationships end. Work changes. These transitions are rarely smooth and never go off without a hitch. More often they are violent, abrupt shifts that shock us and situations blow up unexpectedly, rapidly disintegrate and leave us reeling.

All of that, any of that, can be extremely disconcerting. But I'm reminded of a universal truth, and those are universal truths because they remain true without fail. It is easy to work when times are good and nothing challenges you. It is harder to do when times are hard and everything challenges you. But in which do you grow more? In which do you have most to say, to share, to give through your work? In which does absolute honesty and integrity—purpose—most sustain you and remind you who you are, why you're here and why you've made the choices you've made?

Tough times bring tough reactions. Many of my fellow writers will feel hostile at conditions and repressed anger will surface. Others will slide into depression and sadness will envelope them. They'll feel unable to cope and as if they've failed. All of these are valid emotions and yet none of them are productive or constructive or in anyone's best interests. Negativity breeds negativity. Like attracts like. And falling into step with these things will bring more of the same heaping down on their heads.

In a profession where you hear no so much more often than yes. Where you hear "bad" news so much more often than "good" news. Where you hear war stories far more than ones of dreams coming true. It is impossible to dodge all of those negative bullets. Impossible. To avoid mortal injury, you need thick skin and heavy armor.

You will take hits. To absorb them and stay healthy—physically, mentally, and spiritually—make sure your own arsenal is full. Purpose. Honesty with yourself and others. Openness about your work, your reasons for doing it.

You can fight the realities of your situation, deny they exist, invest your energy in railing at the injustice of it all. A little of that might be healthy now and then. But none of it is healthy for long, and none of it changes anything. What is, is.

Recognize that, accept that with grace, and then look for constructive ways to deal with it.

When you do, amazing things happen. You don't ride emotional roller coasters, you stay balanced. You don't slide into the negativity abyss and spend months clawing and crawling your way out of it—you see it and sidestep it. And because you're looking at the situation with absolute honesty and integrity, your intentions are focused, your purpose clear. And those things work miracles in your life. Those things bring about lasting change.

Actively participating in these transformations, you remain centered and peaceful, and you learn to trust the process. Everything has cycles, seasons, its own time. Change is inevitable and that's a good thing. Not always easy, but ever important.

Change opens new doors and windows and shines light into hidden crawl spaces. It exposes new roots and sprouts new seedlings. Growth is good. Not always without pain—(remember when you were a kid, those leg pains from your bones stretching)—but always with new opportunities and benefits for those who seek them.

And so today I begin my day, focused on acceptance and grace, openness, and look to all the potential this day holds. All the possibilities for purpose. And I wonder how Dr. Morgan Cabot is starting her morning, and how you are starting yours...

❧Bonus 4❧
LOSING IS WINNING?

Daring ideas are like chessmen moved forward. They may be beaten, but they may start a winning game. -Goethe

I came across the above quote this morning, and I have to say that it suits my mind-set at this moment so well, it's almost spooky.

This is November, and as those who've been with me awhile know, that is my renewal month. The time when I look back at the past year and review all that's happened—and what hasn't—and reassess and plan for the year ahead.

A great deal of the month was taken up with two projects. A proposal that had to be redone and a YA (young adult) idea that just nagged the spit out of me and wouldn't turn me loose.

And so it's been an unusual November for me. One in which I've worked on a total of five different projects—a mainstream novel, a series of YA novels, a Bombshell novel trilogy, and two nonfiction projects, one of which has a new pub date of January 2006!

Busy times. Busy times. But also daring times—and why the quote above snagged my interest.

It is no surprise to anyone writing that were are in a tough-time period. Those cycle so few are in panic-mode, but I have to tell you. These cycles have what can be wonderful perks—if you have an open mind.

You can develop this attitude about what you're writing. You can be more willing to take bigger risks. You can throw caution to the wind and write EXACTLY what you want to write

I mean, if your income is reduced due to cycles in market conditions, then it's really not drastic to step out on a limb and do something dramatically different. Something you've wanted to do for whatever reason but held back because things were going great guns on the financial front and you didn't want to take a tumble.

But now, well, you tell yourself, why not? Why not step out on the limb? Give that book of the heart the time and focus to bring it about? Why not do that which only earning money has stopped you from doing?

Big risks mean big successes or big failures. But you know what I've discovered. The failure is not taking the risks. In not doing that which you feel driven or inspired or hungry to do.

What this means—my little tidbit of wisdom gleaned for the day—is that there is no failure in trying anything you feel driven or compelled or inspired to write. Just do it. There is only failure in burying the desire to do it.

I think this is a critical point. One I must ponder today, and likely many days. Failure is not doing that which means much to you. Success is doing that which means much to you.

And so the absence of money, or the diminishment of money can actually be liberating and gaining riches. Money gets out of the way.

Now isn't that an interesting take? Mmm, definitely need to ponder more on this—after I get the final proofing done on *One Way To Write a Novel*. That's the project for today.

∽Bonus 5∾
LIFE INTERRUPTS

Yesterday I received no less than four messages from writers who are having a hard time getting going on a new project right now. And in each of them, the author was despairing that it was a sign of hard times to come. To those authors, and others like them who didn't email me, I say this:

It's a sign of the season, the added things that must be done, the extra above and beyond social engagements, kids' activities, etc. This is the season of more. More to do, more going on. And you're impacted whether or not you celebrate Christmas because those with whom you interact are in more season, too.

So cut yourself a little slack, don't despair, and don't see the difficulty in getting going on a new project as anything more than this is not a time that is conducive to focus and concentration.

Many writers don't schedule deadlines this time of year, or writing at all. They use this time to recoup the previous year and to plan ahead for the next year. They clean out their offices, their closets, and do things that tend to stack up and be ignored when you're in create-mode. Some ignore the office completely and totally envelop themselves in the celebrations of the season, doing all of the things that can only be done then, and things writers don't want to stop writing to do at other times.

Splintered focus is a challenge for everyone, writer or not, during the season. Recognize and accept it, and relax. Consider it a time for refilling the creative well. That's important work!

Mostly, just be gentle with yourself. Added stress and tension runs hand in hand with holidays. The cure for it is in simple things: laughter, patience, acceptance.

❧Bonus 6❧
SUNSHINE, CEMETERIES, AND DIAMONDS

Some days are diamonds. This day is definitely one. You know, you often wonder if the things you do have a positive effect, and you so hope that they do. And every now and then, you're fortunate enough to know the truth—regardless of what it is. If you are having a positive impact, then your instincts on what you're doing are affirmed. And if not, you have an opportunity to change, to take added steps and actions to become a positive influence.

For me, the desire to be a positive influence came early. Unusual things can be the inspiration for us setting the course of our lives. For me, it was a headstone in a cemetery. The grave belonged to a woman, and on it, her family had written: "She was the Sunshine of our Lives."

I was very young, but I remember well standing there and thinking, I hope when I die, someone feels that way about me.

You would think, being so young, that this little incident wouldn't have a great impact. That being a kid, I'd forget. But I never did. It became an aspiration at soul level, and remains one today.

Being the sunshine doesn't mean being the proverbial Little Mary Sunshine. At least, not to me. It does mean shining light into darkness. Helping those you can to find the path to light when they're lost in the dark. Doing what you can to leave the world more hopeful than when you entered it. It means looking out and seeing the needs of others as well as looking in and seeing your own. Caring about others, and noticing the little things. Life is in those little things.

I'm grateful today for that walk through that cemetery. And I wonder: If back then I had seen that saying printed anywhere other than on a headstone, would it have had the same impact on me? I doubt that it would. The end of life is the ultimate "You can do no more here" notice. From the moment of death onward, you're perceived by others' memories of you and no more.

I guess if we all had warnings that we were going to die in x number of days or months, then we could prepare and be light-bearers then. But we don't know when death will claim us, and when you really think about it, for this purpose, it's just as well. You can't cram a lifetime of interactions with others into a few days or months. These types of memories start as soon as you begin interacting with others and continue until your last breath.

Today, a good friend, Debra Webb, sent me a dedication that will be in her June 06 Bombshell novel. I was stunned to see my name there, and to read her comments about why she'd dedicated this book to me. I was so touched and right then, I had to stop and pray that I live long enough and smart enough to become the person she believes I am.

Deb's words had the same impact on me that my mother always had. She believed the best, saw the best, encouraged the best. The ultimate, unconditional faith. And because she did, I sought it. There's such amazing power conveyed in belief!

That's the point I wanted to share. There is humility and fulfillment in attempting to be light, and there is power in belief. In yourself, your spouse and kids. In those you work with, and in your friends—like my diamond, Deb.

৯Bonus 7৯
BALANCE: WRITING
AND LIFE'S OBLIGATIONS

Q. I am a new author, under contract for my first novel to be published early in 2006. My publisher is interested in my second novel as well. I am a wife and mother, homeschool teacher, and my husband and I are in full-time ministry. My question is this, how does one find their flow and balance between all of life's obligations? I have reprioritized my responsibilities over and over to the point that I become frustrated.

You have a full plate, that's for sure, but take heart because most writers do. It goes with the territory—to have much to say, one must experience much.

I suggest a list. On it you add everything that must be done and assign it a priority. Start with the most critical, and work your way down the list. This way, even if you only get halfway, the most urgent things get done first.

Secondly, understand that so long as you are a wife and parent you're going to have interruptions. So long as you home-school, you're going to have teaching as a high priority that interrupts the writing. So long as you reach out to help others through your ministry, you're going to have high-priority inserts, dealing with the needs of others. Accept this and don't become frustrated by it.

Remember that you have higher priorities and you can only see a small segment of your lifetime canvas at one time. So things that might seem important now are tiny droplets of paint on that canvas. Everything goes back to why you're here—and I'd say by your listing of what you're doing, your jobs are significant.

So when you sit down to write and you're hit with a barrage of challenges, read this little list:

Not everyone can or will listen to others who are in trouble, having a hard time, hurting, or lost. Not everyone can or will reach out to help them, trying their best to be constructive, realistic, and positive. You can. This is a gift and it bears an obligation. One you can fulfill or you wouldn't have the gift

2. Not everyone can or will teach children. The responsibility is great. You're shaping minds *and* hearts, teaching them to think with both and you're preparing them to take their place in the world. This is an awesome gift and an amazing opportunity reserved to those among us who can be trusted to understand that the principles they teach and the teachings they share can shape the lives of these children, their friends and families and their children. The ripple of lives touched grows forever. You have been trusted to do this. That's an amazing amount of faith entrusted in your abilities and quite a statement about your capabilities. Remember that when you feel taxed. Few can shape the future and minds as you are doing. Remember the ripple.

3. Your obligations in the ministry are self-evident and you well know their worth. You also know that there is no convenient time for the writing interruptions that come as part and parcel of it. Offering aid or comfort to someone grieving, someone who is without hope, someone who is struggling under a burden they're convinced they cannot bear—well, you know the value of what you do here and certainly don't need for me to tell you how much more important those things are than is writing an extra page or two today. In this, in your writing, it's all about touching people. When you're weary, remember your special place in these persons' lives. You might be the only person on the planet that they feel safe or able to talk to about their trials. That matters.

My point is that these other things you're doing are all significant and all of them carry time requirements—scheduled and unscheduled—but all of them do help you in your writing, too. The experiences are fodder. The events are fodder. The unexpected twists and turns that come up—all fodder.

You can't turn your back on these others things in your life that you've built. They're all important. What you can do is change your mindset, accepting that some days you just won't get as much done on your writing as you'd like. But that doesn't mean that you can't get anything done.

Now, I've mentioned the priority list. Let's look at a couple other tips that could help:

1. You didn't mention the ages of the children, but they're home-schooled and that says they're old enough to help you with chores. Put a chore list on the fridge. Everyone works from the list. (If they're small and what's done isn't perfect, so what? Neither are we. Imperfect works just fine.)

2. Establish a quiet time at home every day. It can be 30 minutes, an hour, two hours. Whatever best works for you and the kids. I used to set the timer on the stove. Until it went off, no one talked, no TV, no noise whatsoever. The kids didn't have to nap, but they had to read. This was "alone" time, and they could think or do anything approved, but it had to be without sound. This was my writing time, and I'll tell you, it's amazing how much you can get done in a short amount of time when you know it's coming and you've got to produce. (No phone calls during quiet time, either. And if an emergency one comes in, then quiet time starts after the crisis is settled.)

3. Buy a little handheld recorder. You'll be free to multi-task. As you're driving, doing household chores, record your next scene or chapter. It's easier to transcribe in a busy environment than it is to create in one. I have a friend who writes three books a year on the drive to and from work. (It's 20-25 minutes.) So don't underestimate what can be done in short spurts.

4. Schedule your deadlines allowing for your life. Some writers will cram deadlines so close together that they have no time away from their desks and no lives and that leaves them out of balance (it's all about harmony within and balance) and frustrated. So simply schedule added time. If you have no idea how long it takes you to write a book (in normal living), then start a time sheet.

I use a time sheet on every book I write because things change around here, and what I need to write a book changes with things. Anyway, on this sheet track:

Date (seasons, holidays—all can impact and you need to know this when gauging)

Time (time of day impacts. Some are more productive at specific times.)

Focus (jot a note of what you worked on—chapter/scene)

Pages (note your progress. Ex. "112-117")

+ or - (+6 = net gain of 6 pages. You could go back and edit previous work. This lets you know what you did and so you again can gauge your time accurately.)

Okay. This will give you a clue how long it's taken you to write this book and how much time you spent editing what you'd written. That will NOT be the same for every book. Some novels come to us full-blown, some come as we write them. The point is, regardless of how they've come, the majority of the books I've written have been written within 20 hours of each other. I've had the exceptions, where I've written an entire novel in 2 weeks, and where I've worked on one for 5 years (and still am not satisfied with it).

But having an idea of about what it takes, you know how to set your deadlines and about what you need to produce to make this work for you. That's the key. Knowing what you need.

Now your life is pretty full, and this next recommendation might seem a little silly, but I'm telling you, I've been where you are (sans the home-schooling and plus the taking care of a diabetic mother) it is not silly, it is critically important. Take 30 minutes each day for yourself. Meditate, exercise, take a bubble bath. Do whatever it is that centers you and makes you feel serene and calm and at peace. Treat this time as if it is sacred—it is—because it nourishes you so that you can then meet the needs of others without being depleted. And know that if you do not do this you will deplete. Expect frustration to grow and taint all you touch. Expect dissatisfaction, disharmony and even depression. The hungry have to eat, and nurturers have to be nourished to nourish. It's that simple.

Q. How did you do it when you were just beginning? Was it a challenge for you as well?

I've shared with you the things that were most critical to me. The biggest asset is the attitude and that daily dose of self-time. Sometimes it's hard, but you've got to make time for it. Remember, your needs matter, too.

This is a challenge for all writers I know—women and men. We all wear so many hats. The very thing that gives us a wealth of experience to be good writers also taxes our strength because we've so much to do to gain that experience. Attitude. I can't stress it enough. It's the saving grace.

Q. I am passionate about my writing, yet I find that I feel guilty at times when I sit down to create and look around and see things that have not been taken care of, or feel like I'm shutting myself away. I can't seem to let things go in order to write like I should. Is this normal?

Absolutely, yes, it is normal. Totally and completely. Working past it requires a revision in perspective.

What are the consequences of...

The beds not being made up? The dishes not being done? The car not being washed? The lawn being mowed tomorrow rather than today? Running a bunch of errands at once rather than making two or three trips?

There are always things to be done. No one ever finishes, and I'll bet if you took a survey at any cemetery in the country from those who've passed on, you'd find they all left unfinished work. It's the nature of life. If we completed everything today, what would get us out of bed tomorrow?

So we have to think about importance. Yes, clean sheets are important. But an unmade bed isn't, and if you're bothered by it, close the door.

Look at those things making you feel guilty. Odds are high 9/10ths of them haven't earned the privilege but are tied up in your perspective of what a good wife, mother, woman does or doesn't do. I can tell you that before I started writing, my house was in perfect order. Everything had its place, and it was in it. Not even the kids left water spots on the bathroom faucets.

After I started writing, I got to looking at that, and wondered what the heck I'd been doing. People *live* here. It's a home, not a hotel. And then things like comfort and happy atmosphere became far more important to me. The bath faucets are cleaned, but who gives a spit if they've got water spots on them? Life in the house is more important than this kind of thing.

So get comfortably messy and ditch the guilt. It doesn't serve a constructive purpose. You'll be happier, and I can tell you from experience, your family will be much, much happier.

I hope that this helps—and as always if you've questions or want to discuss something further, just yell.

≪Bonus 8 ≫
NEW YEAR'S DAY—GRACE

Happy New Year!

2005 ended on a sad note with Alex's death. I won't lie and say it was a wonderful holiday; it wasn't. All the kids were here and they were hurting, too. It's difficult to comfort when your heart is broken.

New Year's Day I did a little of all I hope to do well in 2006. It's one of my (and many others') traditions. I spent a good deal of the day talking to myself about seasons and times and everything having its own. When you lose someone you love, it dredges up all your other loved losses. You can't avoid it. Oh, how I tried, but it's inevitable that you remember every single one, and relive it. The pain in doing so makes your heart hurt so much you can barely breathe.

And so rather than fight the pain, yesterday, I spent time remembering all those I've loved and lost—my parents, my two brothers, my beloved aunt, two dearly loved cousins, all my grandparents, a sweetheart of an uncle, my great-aunt who had more spunk than anyone I've known, my father-in-law and more dear friends than I dare to list here. The number was many, the list lengthy, the pain of each loss again made raw. I started to wonder if this had been a good idea after all. Instead of it getting easier to breathe, I felt the full weight of the heartache of losing them again. But I held the faith that this was the path to acceptance and peace, and remembered on.

Something strange happened. Tears, of course, but also bitter-sweet smiles, and then laughter. In remembering them, I remembered all I loved about them, and I'm not sure how it happened, but the more I thought, the less I felt as if I were wearing my nerves on the outside of my body and my skin within. And the impact of what I logically knew settled into my heart.

Love lives on.

Memories heal.

That's the heart of the other side of grief, the healing part. Oh, it doesn't come all at once, but it does come. The hope in that dulls the pain that has made breathing too hurtful. And that, dear friends, is Grace.

The day after Alex died, all the other deaths ravaged me. There's no polite way to say it, or positive way to frame it. It was horrific. One of my best friends, who knows me at times better than I know myself, stopped by to check on me. I told her I was so tired of losing those I love. I just can't stand losing another one. I just can't stand it. Her eyes filled; she too knows loss, and grief. She didn't offer platitudes. She didn't tell me things would get better, though we both knew they would. She just cried with me.

I said I didn't expect to get hit this hard over Alex. I knew it would hurt. I didn't expect to grieve so deeply. She looked me right in the eye and said, you loved her. To other people, she was just a dog. But not to you. Wisdom shone in her eyes. She'd lost her puppy, Lindsay, four years earlier. Two days after Alex died. She remembered and again felt the losses of her loved ones who've passed on.

Grief recognizes grief. Acknowledges it. Endures it. Survives it. But time isn't what heals; this I know for fact. Not when years later triggers makes it new again, makes you raw again. Only Grace heals wounds. Only Grace.

Love lives on.

Memories heal.

❧Bonus 9 ❧
PLANNING THE YEAR AHEAD, CONTROLLING INCIDENTALS & CHASING TITLES

Typically this time of year, we're all off to a running start with New Year's resolutions. We've laid out our plans and are now busy enacting them.

Whether you call your intentions for 2006 intentions or goals or plans or resolutions, the bottom line is they're a map to what you want to accomplish in the coming year.

If you haven't yet done this, don't despair. There's an in-depth article in the library on the www.vickihinze.com web site, "Why We Need a Plan," that can offer guidance on different aspects of writing you might want to consider for developing your plan, along with an example I use.

Most writers attempt to clear the decks to make getting into the writing as easy as possible—with the fewest life interruptions. That's a good idea, IMHO; I do it myself. But two things nip at the heels of this action:

1. Within a few weeks, all the other incidentals stack up again and

2. Because the incidentals are cleared, we "think" we have more time than we actually do and we either:

    A. Start an additional project or

    B. Volunteer for something.

And then in a few weeks when the incidentals pile up again, we're overwhelmed.

The point of the message is to be careful about taking on new things during the first few weeks of the New Year. Hold off until your desk clutters a little and you get a more realistic view of what this year's "stable" is in your writing world.

I've been asked several times in the last week an efficient way to title books. For some writers, the title is something that can change easily. For others, like me, the title comes and it directs the thrust of the story. I write around the title. So it's critical to have in mind a strong title that can carry the weight of a story.

For example. *Her Perfect Life*, my April book. I imagined and gave a woman all she ever wanted—and then took every single bit of it away from her and forced her to rebuild a new life. In doing so, she discovers its perfection.

You can see that no other title would fit as well as this one. Why? Because the entire story spins around it. It is the story.

Whether you start with a kernel of an idea, character, situation, you translate it to the title and then build from there. You might change it several times during development, but each change will be targeted specifically to this story and these characters.

One suggestion is that before you settle in with a title, run it on bn.com and see if it's been used. If it has, and its been a couple years, you can likely stick with it. If it's been used lately, you might want to change it. Slight alterations work as well as synonyms. When you've got the right cadence, you'll know it; trust your inner ear and your gut.

Titles are often changed, but if you weave the story around yours, and it is ingrained into the book, the odds are greater that you'll keep it.

Remember, those of you who haven't yet set out your plan (intentions/resolutions) for 2006, that it isn't too late. Check out the article in the library, spent an hour with yourself and decide what you want to do. Drifting aimlessly is not a trustworthy mode of transportation on your career path.

↩Bonus 10↪
WHEN LIFE INTERRUPTS

No one likes to have their routine or rhythm interrupted. It's disturbing, throws a person off-stride, irritates and annoys. And then things get really nasty because other obligations don't go away, good fairies don't sweep in and take care of everything, and the disabled person watches her clear desktop disappear and "Do me Next" piles appear and multiply and she can't do one thing about any of it.

The first few days are the roughest because you're still geared into keeping up with everything. Production, promotion, email and other correspondence, research and workshops. You try to work anyway, but soon discover that you just can't do it. Then anger and resentment set in, and eventually you work around to resignation. I wish I could say that this is a graceful acceptance, but the truth is that it is not. It is resignation-on-demand and not by choice, and there's additional resentment at that. "I'm a good person. I work hard, try to help others when I can, do my best to live a life with purpose and all this 'stuff' happens to me that I can't control and I'm sick to death of it. I'm sick to death of being sick."

That is a more accurate depiction of the process. However, when railing against the injustices in life does absolutely nothing to improve the situation—in fact, it grows worse—resentment can't get any stronger, and so other things—ones that you have slowed down long enough (by force, yes, but still you've slowed down) to notice capture your attention and your concentration.

And you begin to think, to ponder things you've not stopped to ponder for a while. You find other ways to communicate, other ways to work, if only in your mind. And you find yourself working on other things—things you have neglected for some time or never before considered. You even find yourself reconsidering and redefining that which you thought was steadfast and certain and it hits you that this interruption has given you an opportunity. One to pause, reflect, reconsider. An opportunity to change something significant.

The resentment falls to the discovery. The interruption provides a new vista. And grateful, if not graceful, acceptance swells. You finally relax, stop worrying and have faith that everything will work out exactly as it is supposed to work out, and accept that this interruption too has purpose. And then something magical happens. It's as if your receptors open wide because you'll be doing something totally unrelated to anything (like sitting in a rocking chair with an empty mind) and suddenly a title pops into your head. You whisper it, letting the syllables roll over your tongue. It interests you, and you repeat it aloud. And in a flash the entire story is clear in your mind. The premise, the characters, the events—and the purpose.

It isn't a story you would have written without the interruption, and yet there is something indistinctly you in it. Something that nudges you, niggles way down deep that this IS your story to tell.

In raw form, you pitch it to your critique partner, unsure of her reaction, which sets your teeth on edge. She loves it; suggests you develop it. You then pitch it to a trusted friend with a closed mouth and keen eye. She gets chills; says go for it. You pitch it to a second trusted friend (it's so different, you need the affirmation before further investing), and that feedback too is overwhelmingly positive. So with raw form vetted, you pitch to your agent, and again get a green light with a little caveat.

All systems are go, and because this isn't your usual, it's also open to being worked on in unusual for you ways. And so you do. You think, you run the movie of it in your mind. You work, but also play, and your limitation brought on by life's interruption doesn't seem so limiting anymore. In a sense, it's liberating.

You ponder that for a time—the liberation—and realize that you've been functioning in a rut. You've been less enthused and more intent on just getting this-or-that done. You also realize that you've been writing more someone else's vision than your own, and because you have, you've enjoyed the work far less and witnessed the magic in it being tamped.

More wake-up calls. And more and more.

And none of them would have had the opportunity to surface had life not interrupted.

I guess the moral of this little post is that sometimes you need to not see to see things most clearly. I guess we need those life interruptions to encourage us to stop and take stock and revisit what we are doing and why, and to either determine our commitment to what we're doing or change things so that we can again be committed.

While I'm still in my little life interruption—predictions are two weeks more—I'm convinced that there are more lessons to be learned in it. For me, the interruption was a little eye surgery complicated by an abrasion. The abrasion requires antibiotic ointment that knocks out vision in my left eye. It's healing, but not yet healed. The right eye is healing from surgery. (This is what happens when goggles worn to bed to protect your eyes slip during sleep and scratch the good eye.) Anyway, I'll be back to normal in short order. For that, I am grateful.

But I am also grateful for the interruption. It's enabled me to take a look at my life and work and reassess. It's enabled me to recommit to the writing and writing only with purpose. It's given me the time and incentive to think.

Isn't it strange? Sometimes you have to temporarily lose your sight to see most clearly...

✄Bonus 11✂
CHANCES

"If you want to be successful, you must either have a chance or take one." —*Author Unknown*

I came across this quote, read it, read on, and stopped cold, then backed up and read it again. "Ain't it the truth," I mumbled to myself, then went on with the day's duties.

But all during the day, the frank honesty in the quote kept coming back to me. I thought of things I'm currently doing that are, well, risky. I thought of a good friend, who is taking on not one but two new businesses for the sheer love them. I thought of a writer who is leaving a very lucrative niche in her writing for one she feels called to write.

These are acts of faith, yes. But they are also acts of courage. People looking chance in the eye and saying, "Yes, I'm going to risk you for something more."

Some wouldn't agree that courage is involved, but from experience, I have to say that it is. It's easy to change directions when things are awful or not as robust as you'd like. It's easy to change when conditions are not meeting your definition of success. Or when the financial benefits are just not what you need.

Under those types of conditions, the difficult thing would be to not change to better your position.

But in the cases mentioned above, situations are not horrible. Needs are not failing to be met. In the cases above, these individuals have redefined what they want or want to accomplish—

their purpose in doing what they're doing. Some are sacrificing income to do it. Others are putting savings on the line. Some are putting their reputation on the table.

When you think about what these people are putting into play, what they're risking, it really makes you think about what has the power to convince you to take these kinds of chances. Not just anything will do; not with risks like these.

I thought about this more and more and continued on with what I was doing, but my mind kept coming back to chances. I've been fortunate in my life, often being presented with the chances I've needed at the time I've needed them. But there have been other times. Ones where I couldn't seem to catch a break with both hands and a net. And yet, in persisting, a chance appeared.

Whether it was created by will and effort or by grace, I can't say. Only that if I hadn't still been seeking it, even though I couldn't see it, I surely would have missed it.

And I guess that's the point in this post. If you need a chance, and one appears, fabulous. If not, don't despair and certainly don't give up. Keep after whatever it is you want enough to take risks. Because a little faith, a little courage, and in those risks, you'll create a chance—or encounter grace.

Either way, that's success.

❧Bonus 12❧
IF IT AIN'T ONE THING...

Sometimes you just have to give in to events taking place around you and laugh. You can rail at the injustice—and get a sore throat. Raise hell and make everyone in your life miserable—and reap the not-so-appealing rewards of that. Or just say, "Okay, then," and roll with the punches—or the flow, whichever you prefer.

Last Thursday, I thought, great. I'm going to get on speed again. Yes, a little more to go on the eyes, but the end of the tunnel is so close, and I can see the screen reasonably well now, which is just fantastic. So I come to my computer with great anticipation, almost as eager to write as my darling husband is for me to write. (Like most writers, I get a wee bit cranky when I'm not creating. Well, okay. A lot cranky.)

Anyway, I was excited. And about two minutes into sitting at my computer and feeling oh-so-comfortable and happy to be there, my computer crashed.

Absolutely reveling in the moment only to get zapped.

You can imagine well enough my initial reaction. (Be kind.) And you can well imagine my secondary reaction, which was full-out panic at all the work I'd lost that wouldn't be recovered. That, naturally led to my third reaction: "Oh, man, am I in trouble here, or what?"

I had to fight despairing, but you know, I really did. And I'm grateful for that. I figured getting all upset wouldn't fix the computer, and what's lost will still be lost, so I might as well just accept it and press on.

So rather than spending the day irked to the nines, I took the computer to the guru, told him to do what he could, and then took a friend to lunch to celebrate her birthday. We ate, laughed, talked and walked through a little shopping village near the beach, and just made a day of it.

No, it didn't resolve the challenge. But I didn't spend a lot of energy on it, either. I had a great time—and the good news came this morning: only bits of stuff were lost. The computer guru worked his magic and was able to recover things precious to me—like the photos.

Rolling with the punch sure took the force out of it—and I got lucky—and some great memories of a good time, too.

I love it when I don't get into my own way and things work out better than expected. Makes for a nice day.

ᚻBonus 13ᚹ
HAPPY BIRTHDAY TO ME

"Human beings, by change, renew, rejuvenate ourselves; otherwise we harden." —Johann Wolfgang Von Goethe

I know women are supposed to hate birthdays. They're supposed to get hyped up about aging and all that, go into a blue funk for about a week (or a month), and eat their way through a couple pounds of chocolate at the nearest candy store. You know, to get "happy" chemical relief into a mourning body that just ain't what it used to be.

But that's all hype created by marketers who want you to feel bad about yourself. Your emotional imbalance is good for their fiscal balance, if you know what I mean.

Sorry to disappoint them, but the truth is I know very few women who obsess over aging. Most consider every year a victory. I went through these ups and downs and I'm still upright. I learned how to do this. I finally got time to do that. Hey, I got a turn this year!!!!

At year's end, we've either been comatose or we've changed a little. We've laughed, we've cried, we've yawned. We've gotten fired up, calmed down, taken in and chilled out—sometimes, all in the same day. The bottom line? We lived.

Living is winning. Some people exist through an entire life, too intimidated of screwing up or making mistakes to live even a moment of it. Now if you're in that boat, you've got something worth worrying about going on. But if you're out there making the trip, scaling the mountains, trudging through the valleys, enjoying a few joys and a few kicks in the gut, then you're doing just fine. Celebrate.

Sore from the journey? Probably. Even Atlas had to shrug, right? Okay, I'll give you that one. The body's got a few more crackle and pops and a few more scars than it did at twenty. But the mind's sharper and that high mileage experience has the soul a lot more at ease. So the balance of power between the physical, emotional and spiritual has shifted and moved a little further inward. Considering the body wears out and gives up and the soul hangs with, isn't that a good thing? Emphasis growing on the part that's everlasting?

I don't know, my friends. I worry about people who are age conscious in the same way I worry about women who are afraid to leave home or be seen in public without makeup. I actually knew a woman once who boasted that her husband had never seen her without lipstick. They'd been married over a decade.

Now I'm not a cruel person, but I am curious, and I didn't ask but I certainly did wonder what she was afraid he'd see. The naked face is a beautiful thing—especially one that's been lived in a little. It's interesting in ways others are not, you know?

It takes heat to temper steel. Time to experience. Years to develop—or become a—character. Our society is rather obsessed with youth. That's not without humor, if you think about it. We're a people who fully appreciates the rich, full-throated smoothness of an aged wine but we spend billions to halt the clock on become aged people.

As for me, I'm celebrating this new year. Maybe I look at this whole aging business differently because I had a brother locked into life as a vegetable for all but five short months of his entire life. Maybe it's because I've had a few close calls and survived them intact. Maybe it's just a genuine appreciation for the different seasons in life. I don't know. It's probably all of that and more.

But I'll tell you something it's not and that's fear or marketing hype convincing me I should be fearful of aging. Each decade has brought new assets and interests, and though I hear all the ads saying I should be thinking about aging and getting obsessed with erasing lines off my face, I believe I'll just keep blowing them off—the ads, not the lines.

The truth is I don't think about age much. And I just picked up a year. No, not because of the birthday. Because I spent the last year thinking I was a year older than I really was. I hear you laughing, but kindly remember that words, not math, is my strong suit.

Okay, so maybe the reason is that I've already spent a year being this age. A two-for-one deal. Hey, now that's victory!

Whatever it is, I'm going to enjoy this coming year. I'm going to be grateful for it and cram it full of fantastic memories. And if I get a new line on my face, well, I'm going to enjoy that, too. These little marks are memories on their own.

The crease at the brow? Oh, getting all three kids in college without declaring bankruptcy. This one, near the mouth? Mike's two wrecks in four weeks—neither his fault, both putting him in high risk. That one, near the eye? Two wars, two men off in them. That one? A daughter in surgery, deepened later by her delivering a baby.

You know, when you get down to it, the face is a road map of a life. And some marketing mogul wants me to erase that? No, I think not.

My birthday wish: May all of you realize your dreams, hold in your hearts that which makes you happy, and in the mirror see your road map reflecting a full life well lived.

◈Bonus 14◈
LOST TREASURES

Last weekend at a writer's conference, I was asked about the books that didn't sell, and I realized that I haven't discussed those much. So I thought I'd address my views on that for the writers among us, and for curious readers.

First, I know no writers who don't have projects that didn't get published. Or any writers who after they're published don't continue to add new projects to their unpublished list. Why does that happen? Well, you might hit the market at the wrong time with a proposed project. For example, a story of someone hijacking a plane and flying it into a building right around 9/11. Or you might hit on a topic that makes people squeamish—like poisoning of food supplies on the borders when that's just come into focus on the nation's radar. You might hit a sore subject, or one that a major writer has just contracted to write for the same publisher.

The reasons are as varied as writers, and often they have nothing to do with the quality of the work but everything to do with marketing.

So when this happens, what does the writer do with the work?

The truth is that it depends—and it'd be easier to tell you what the writer doesn't do with it. S/he doesn't toss it and forget it.

If the story and characters are so compelling as a unit that the writer can't bear to separate them, then odds are high s/he will shelve the project until such time as the market is more receptive. But what I've most noted is that characters have far more than one story in them. Just as we, in our lives, have more than one compelling event we can share with one another. And so an idea for a new novel comes along, or the germ of one, and before the writer knows what hit her, a former character jumps in and claims his or her space in it.

So the writer weighs that character in this story and often finds that character is the perfect character for it. So the material and character's internal and external conflicts that were used in the old story become the spine of the new story. And before you know it, you've got a different book with solid characters, solid conflicts and a new project.

I've pulled characters from several different proposals and created a new project with them, sold the new project, and then brought in elements from the old project in a subsequent, related book. Times change, the market changes, and what didn't find a comfortable market home earlier can later.

Early on, I wrote a lot of complete manuscripts that weren't published. I had a penchant for mixing genres—four or five of them—and that made them difficult to sell because they didn't fit neatly into any defined genre. Where would they go on the bookshelf in the bookstore? That was a marketing challenge, but it sure made for fun writing!

Now, in many cases, those marketing lines have softened. There are defined sub-genres where many of these works do fit. There are established reader bases for these types of books. It's a whole different world, and these projects now have a place in it.

The writing has changed a good deal since those days, as it does for any writer who writes over a period of time. But those things are the mechanics, the craft, and they can be honed.

I've often been told that early works are most original. I believe that's true, because the writer is writer for the sheer love of it, unencumbered by anything else. That's a privilege, though many writers don't realize it until they start feeling the weight of those encumbrances. Yet writers can recapture that early enthusiasm in borrowing from or reworking those early stories—those lost treasures.

And the writer can also maintain a trust with him or herself. One where s/he vows to never write a book s/he doesn't love. That, too, is a treasure—and it's one the writer should never allow to be lost.

❧Bonus 15❧
WHEN I GROW UP...

For the past decade or so, I've had a sign on my office wall that reads: WHEN I GROW UP, I WANT TO BE A FAIRY GODMOTHER.

Now before you give in to a hard belly-laugh or a fit of giggles, pause a second and think about it. Can you imagine a more fulfilling job or life than one dedicated to helping people work through their challenges constructively and assisting them in making their dreams come true?

I do what I can in my ways. Most are secret and will remain so. A few are open and those who are of a mind know what they are. The rest don't really care, so it's insignificant. But what is significant is that we don't have to wait to pursue this types of wishes, hopes or desires.

A few weeks ago, I had a chat with my son about happiness. There are always times in life when it seems elusive, and times when we feel we're on a perpetual hunt that will never end. But the truth is that happiness isn't something we chase. We all have it, just as we have that divine spark some call a soul and others refer to by different names.

Happiness is our right and we own it. But like everything else in life, it's subject to our own free will. We choose to be happy— or not to be happy. And so my advice to my son was to make a conscious decision every morning on awakening, before putting his feet on the floor. For that day, choose to be happy. For that day, claim your divine right.

Claiming happiness doesn't mean that you won't be confronted with challenges. It does mean that when you're confronted with them you'll be in a better state to deal with them in a manner that doesn't drag you through hell. It doesn't mean you'll fake a perpetual sense of joy that you don't really feel.

Claiming your right to be happy is an attitude. It's accepting that wherever you are on your path, you have faith that it is exactly where you're supposed to be. It's knowing that no matter what happens, you can get through it without going into self-destruct mode. It's believing in you.

And once you believe in you, then you take better care of you. You give yourself the same respect and care and nurturing that you give others. It's amazing how few of us do that. We break our necks and bust our asses to do for others, but hesitate or feel guilty about doing for ourselves. That mindset embraces a lack of self-respect, and each of deserves better—and we can have it. We need only claim it.

Once we do that, claim care for ourselves, we look at things more gently, and that enables us to then really care about others. It's at that point that we can do most for ourselves and them.

I was reminded last night, by watching an episode of *Extreme Makeover, Home Edition*—I so hope I got the program name right. Just in case, it's hosted by Ty, formerly of Trading Spaces. Anyway, I was reminded by this program that one doesn't have to wait for optimum conditions to help others. One can do so at any time.

This was an "After the Storm" segment that followed the life of a woman after Hurricane Katrina. She's an African-American woman known in her community as Big Mama. Before the storm, Big Mama and her three young sons lived in a fish market. They slept on the floor. Then Hurricane Katrina hit and Big Mama proved she had a big heart.

She pulled out food and began cooking. And she cooked, and cooked, and cooked. She fed as many as two thousand, and she worked with the children to make their after-the-storm lives less traumatic. And she became the stabilizer in her community, the one who led by example, showing others the way back to a more normal life.

Also from
Vicki Hinze
&
Spilled Candy Books

The Prophet's Lady
A Novel of Reincarnation and Love
Through the Ages

(originally published in 1996
by Kensington Books
as *Maybe This Time*)

A Re-Published Treasure from
Spilled Candy Traditional
(www.spilledcandytraditional.com)

One Way to Write a Novel

New from
Spilled Candy Books for Writers
(www.spilledcandytraditional.com)

ORDER FORM

Dear Spilled Candy Books for Writers,

I'd like to order

_____ copies of ONE WAY TO WRITE A NOVEL @ $14.95 each
_____ copies of THE COMMON SENSE GUIDE @ $14.95 each
_____ copies of THE PROPHET'S LADY @ $21.95 each

I am enclosing………………………………………..$_____

Plus shipping ($4 of rhe 1st book, then $1 per book).$_____

Plus Sales tax (Florida residents—6%)………………..$_____

Total amount enclosed…………………………………..$_____

Check / Money order   payable to *Spilled Candy Books*

NAME:_____

ADDRESS:_____

_____

EMAIL or PHONE:_____

___ Mastercard   ___Visa   ___ AmEx   __ Discover

CARD #_____EXP DATE_____/_____

3-DIGIT VERIFICATION NUMBER (right of #) _____

SIGNATURE:_____

Mail to Spilled Candy Books, P O Box 5202, Niceville FL 32578 or fax to 850/897-

ORDER FORM

Dear Spilled Candy Books for Writers,

I'd like to order

_____ copies of ONE WAY TO WRITE A NOVEL @ $14.95 each
_____ copies of THE COMMON SENSE GUIDE @ $14.95 each
_____ copies of THE PROPHET'S LADY @ $21.95 each

I am enclosing..$_____

Plus shipping ($4 of rhe 1st book, then $1 per book).$_____

Plus Sales tax (Florida residents—6%)....................$_____

Total amount enclosed..$_____

Check / Money order   payable to *Spilled Candy Books*

NAME:_____

ADDRESS:_____

_____

EMAIL or PHONE:_____

___ Mastercard   ___Visa   ___ AmEx   __ Discover

CARD #_____EXP DATE____/_____

3-DIGIT VERIFICATION NUMBER (right of #) _____

SIGNATURE:_____

Mail to Spilled Candy Books, P O Box 5202, Niceville FL 32578 or fax to 850/897-

Printed in the United States
55966LVS00003B/218